I hope you enjoy the ride and the read!

Driving From Here to WOW!
Looking at Life through the Windshield

Dave Armstrong

Dave Armstrong "wow!"

Dedication

Dedicated to my brother Mark...
a fallen hero.

He is forever etched in my mind
and in my heart.

Acknowledgements

In sports, coaches talk about team effort. Certainly this effort would not have been possible without the help of my teammates.

Two women in particular were invaluable in their expert council, and I'll forever be in their debt.

Claudia Tally was my main editor. Her guidance and advice from the start of this project right through to the finished product was instrumental in getting this to print. She was like a coach on the sidelines encouraging me to continue. At times, cheering me on. At other times, nudging me in a different direction. I can't thank her enough. She was with me on this project from the very start. She also was there at the end making sure it came out in print just the way we hoped it would.

As a sportscaster, I'm used to talking for a living. Writing is a different venue altogether. Mary Dillard made sure the punctuation was correct while being mindful of not changing the text from the conversational style I envisioned. She was kind enough to find the humor in all the appropriate spots. Although I'm sure she found some humor of her own in my feeble attempts to place comma's in their proper place.

My family is owed both thanks and an apology. Most of the writing for this book took place during an already hectic football and basketball schedule. This made life pretty crazy in our home. Their patience during this time was off the charts. We have always been each others greatest cheerleaders, and I appreciate their support and encouragement more and more each day.

I'd also like to thank the dozens of friends and sports personalities mentioned in the following pages. In particular, Reid Gettys. I appreciate his friendship, his forward, and his car you'll read about in Chapter Six.

Thanks also to all the great people at Book Surge. Since this is my first book, their guidance through the publishing process was priceless. Their help took this book from my laptop to the printed page.

Forward

Drive instead of fly, are you nuts? That's why God put wings on airplanes, right? Why would anyone in their right mind *choose* to take a road trip in a car?

I blame it on a combination of being a native Texan and on commuting an hour to work each morning. But to me, there is only one thing in the world worse than driving, and that is driving or in my case, I should say trying to drive...in the snow! How anyone who lives in the north (defined in Texas as anyone who lives north of Dallas) can navigate an automobile on an icy road is beyond me. The mere thought of "black ice" sends me skidding off into a ditch.

Over the last several years as I have traveled around the Big 12 working basketball games for ESPN, I have come up with the perfect solution for my "ice-phobia". If there is cold weather in the forecast, I simply call Dave Armstrong to meet me at the airport and I let him do the driving! Even if you are like me and you hate being in a car, a road trip riding shotgun with Armstrong for a couple of hours is a blast! An endless supply of stories, laughs that will have your sides hurting, and inevitably, an open and candid conversation about "real life" issues and challenges…are all included at no extra charge.

As a litigation attorney by day, I am obligated to disclose to you that I am a biased witness. In my opinion, if Dave Armstrong is not the best announcer in the business, he is certainly on an extremely short list! Dave is the consummate professional; meticulously prepared, insightful and most importantly, he realizes that it is always "just a game." Whether you are announcing a game with him, listening to him announce a game or maybe just navigating another icy highway, if you can't have fun with Dave, there is something seriously flawed with you that no book can help! I consider Dave to be a coach, a cheerleader, a mentor and above all else, a life long friend.

So, if you are ready, let me invite you on a different kind of road trip. Pretend like the roads are iced over, grab a cup of coffee (don't forget your spill proof lid), **clean your shoes off,** slide into the shotgun seat, buckle up and get ready for one of the most enjoyable road trips you will ever take!

P.S. I feel obligated to provide a preemptory strike to any personal ridicule that Chapter Six might invoke. After my wife read Chapter Six, not only has she refused to ride in "Big Green", now she won't even let me park him on the driveway. Needless to say, this has not been very convenient; perhaps it is time for its *annual* wash!

Reid Gettys
Exxon Mobil Corporation
Litigation Counsel

Contents

Chapter One
I Love to Drive!

I love to drive! I suppose since I'm from the Motor City of Detroit, it's in my DNA. Cars have always been a big part of my life. My hometown's welfare depended on the automobile. As a kid in the sixties, most of us could tell you the make, model and year of virtually every car on the road. Of course, this was long before the great influx of imports. Sure, you'd occasionally see a Volkswagen or a Mercedes. But most of the cars on the road back then were American cars from General Motors, Chrysler, American Motors or Ford. Not only built tough, but also built right here in the U.S. of A. Built by dads and uncles and cousins. It was very unusual if you grew up in Detroit and didn't have some relative who worked for one of the "Big Four." Most of the cars bustling down the highway were made in my town. And we knew them all.

In fact, it turned into a little game on the street corner among the boys in the neighborhood. Someone would drive by; and if it was your turn, you'd have to call out the right name and year of the car. For instance, "That's a '61 Chevy Corvette." Or, "That's a '65, no wait, a '64 and-a-half Ford Mustang." It was pretty embarrassing to get it wrong, and we rarely did. You'd look for subtle differences in each car. A change in the fender design, or maybe different taillights. Two cars might look the same to the untrained eye, but we could tell a '61 from a '62. Now I have a rough time just coming up with the name of the company, let alone the make and the year. About the only one you really notice is the model you happen to be driving.

Son of a Firefighter

My dad is a retired firefighter from the city of Detroit. He loved his job. Just as I love mine. He tells me he misses the adrenalin rush of entering a burning building. Unlike my dad, I fall far short in the bravery department. I don't even like tall ladders. But our common bond is that search for adventure.

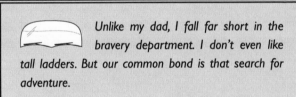

Unlike my dad, I fall far short in the bravery department. I don't even like tall ladders. But our common bond is that search for adventure.

For many years, before he became a chief, my dad drove the squad truck from Headquarters near Cobo Hall in downtown Detroit. He had to maneuver that thing at high speeds around hairpin corners right in the heart of the city. Every now and then he'd take us kids on a "fire run." In our family car, he would turn corners a little faster, speed a little. Looking back, I'm sure he wasn't going too much over the limit, but it was a great thrill to go on one of these rides. There were also those times when we were rambling down a road out in the country where he'd let me sit on his lap and "drive." I'm sure he never took his hand off the wheel, but it made me feel all grown up. Yes, it's safe to say I've always like driving.

A Defining Moment--The Oregon Trail

When I was twelve, my mom and dad decided we were going on a vacation to visit relatives way out in Oregon. We didn't have the money to fly, so this meant a cross-country trip in our family station wagon. Ours was a '65 Ford Ranch Wagon. Blue. I know what you're thinking. No, it didn't have the wood paneling on the outside. This baby was "stripped down." No power steering, no power brakes, not even power windows. Just the basics. Not one single option. Certainly no cruise control or leather seats. No entertainment package like we have in cars or SUVs today. We didn't have the luxury of watching movies or playing video games. Our video game was looking out the window. There was the license plate game, or the alphabet game. And singing. Lots of really bad, off-key sing- ing. One thing in common with today's passengers though, plenty of "Are we there yet?" naggings.

I want you to get a clear picture of this blue beau- ty we took cross-country. Since it didn't come with any "factory" extras, my dad decided to "soup it up." My dad was, and still is, a very handy man. He can use a scrap of this or that and fashion something workable. It seems like he can fix almost anything. Certainly not a skill that was passed on to his son.

> *My dad was, and still is, a very handy man. He can use a scrap of this or that and fashion something workable.*

My kids still laugh about the "Soap Box Derby" we entered with a car honed by a tree saw and some sandpaper. I'm not kidding! Needless to say, we didn't win the race. In fact our car, and that's a loose definition of the word, defied the laws of gravity. Much to the amazement of everyone watching, our little chunk of wood on wheels actually stopped halfway down the hill. No one had ever witnessed an occurrence like that before. The worst part is, I forced my son, who is two years younger than his older sister, to use the same hunk of balsa when it was his turn. You guessed it; we got stuck on the slotted slope again. Isn't that the classic definition of insanity? Doing the same thing over again expecting a different result. All the rocket scientists in the neighborhood with their fancy models got a pretty good chuckle out of our car and its repeat performance. I think my kids are still psychologically scarred from the experience.

The problem with being so crafty, like my dad, is sometimes you don't know when you've turned that piece of junk not into maybe something great but just more junk. First, he installed an AM/FM radio with an extra speaker in the back. He didn't install a speaker that sat flush with the roof. No, he made a speaker box from some scrap lumber lying around the garage. The speaker hung down from the roof about six inches. With razor sharp corners. You need to have this background; it will come into play later in the story. He also installed an air conditioning unit that did a pretty good job for the passengers in the front seat. A little help for the passengers in the middle seat. Virtually no coolant at all to the ones in the "way back." This is where my brother and I were forced to sit.

Instinctively knowing that his sons may get hot back there on a trip across the desert in the middle of the summer, my dad came up with the brilliant idea of "tinting" the windows. Of course this was a do-it-yourself project. He got some of the darkest green tint known to man. Think evergreen and go five shades darker than that. To apply this "tint," he had to be very careful to roll it on just right to avoid getting "bubbles" on the windows. It was stuck directly to the glass like wallpaper.

 For the longest time, I thought everything in America was a bubbly green.

My dad is resourceful, and very handy. But he wasn't particularly careful on this project. We had more "bubbles" than a Lawrence Welk convention. For the longest time, I thought everything in America was a bubbly green. Not just trees or grass, but cows and cactus and every other car on the highway. Everything.

One other thing I should point out about the conditions of the "way back." There were no seat belts. We didn't need them because there was no actual seat back there. You couldn't get away with that today. I hope Ralph Nadar doesn't read this; he'd probably find a way to sue my dad for something. I hope there's a statute of limitations. My brother, who was five at the time, and I sat on a metal floor so hard it would take our circulation away. And still, despite the living conditions of our vehicle, we were somehow excited about this trip. We should have known better. I've often thought of the blank stares I'd get from my own kids if I asked them to hop back there. Different times. But certainly not simpler.

On this sojourn was my dad, who did most of the driving. My grandmother, my mom's mom. She had to sit in the front riding "shotgun." Something about carsickness if she sat anywhere else in the vehicle. My mom and my sister sat in the middle row. While my brother and I got a "green" view of America from the rear cargo hold. My sister slept through 95 percent of the trip. I think that of the seventeen states we went through, she saw maybe two. Part of Colorado and our final destination, Oregon. My mom was the official "navigator" and historian. She literally kept a journal of the entire trip. So you could check my account against hers to see how far I've strayed from the truth. My older sister was getting married later that summer, so she didn't make this memorable journey. And, oh yes, one more thing. I've left the names out to protect the innocent.

So off we went from Michigan to Oregon. Four thousand, eight hundred and fifty-six miles round-trip in "Old Blue." We would usually drive between 12 and 14 hours a day. By the end of each day my brother and I would need a blood transfusion to feel our legs again. It took four days of this to reach our final destination. The trip was pretty uneventful until we reached the beautiful "green" Rocky Mountains. I had never seen anything like them before. (Or since for that matter.) To get a little better "view," my brother and I would scratch away at the "tint" with our fingernails, trying to etch out a better vantage point. All the while being careful not to let dad see us ruining his handiwork. It's really breathtaking to take in the majesty of the Rockies out of a small slit of daylight.

Up in the mountains, the roads got a bit curvy and elevated. And guardrail-less. This totally freaked out my grandma. Around each and every corner, she would yell at my dad to go slower and be more careful. "Oh Bill, oh Bill! Watch out! You're getting too close to the edge!" (Sorry, Dad, I tried to keep your name out of this.) For the better part of a day she would hold up a Kleenex box to block her view while screaming at every turn. If you've ever stood near a roller coaster at an amusement park, you know the sound. Only Grandma was louder. She sounded like Beverly Sills warming up backstage for an upcoming aria. Of course this constant barrage of shrieking scales coming from the seat next to him only made my dad want to take Grandma on a "fire run." He didn't, but I'm sure he wanted to.

Since my brother and I had no way of strapping ourselves in, we would sway back and forth with each hairpin curve. This meant having to dodge the head-slicing speaker hovering inches over our heads. That thing took a pound of flesh from our scalp before we were out of the Rockies. My mom left that part out of her journal, but it's true.

The next day, Grandma had trouble with setting the alarm clock. Time zones and such. So we were back on the road at 3 in the morning. Maybe two hours of sleep at the hotel. I've always wondered about the wisdom of putting a sixty something, sometimes-forgetful older lady in charge of the clock.

> *My dad, calmly at first, asked her to please hush. This did about as much good as standing at the bottom of Niagara Falls and asking the water to stop cascading over the cliff.*

Anyway, on our way through Montana, we noticed they had open grazing. No fences for the cattle. Another golden opportunity for Grandma to freak. "Bill, watch out for the cows! Bill, the cows! They're gonna run out on the road!" She would yell this at the top of her lungs about every five seconds. My dad, calmly at first, asked her to please hush. This did about as much good as standing at the bottom of Niagara Falls and asking the water to stop cascading over the cliff. Of course, all this frenzy at high speed sent my brother and me into a tizzy. "Please Dad, don't kill the 'green' cows," we would yell from the cheap seats. Finally, my dad could take it no longer. We went from 70 to zero in a flash. Leaving tire tracks all over I-90. The force of this stop catapulted my brother and I from the "way back" to the middle seat with my mom and sister, barely waking her up in the process. But not before the killer speaker took the final pound of flesh from our scalps. My dad got out of the car. There was no subtlety about this move. It was clear, and it was dramatic. The flair with which he slammed the door behind him might earn an Oscar if this were an act. He stomped across the median. Standing now on the other side of the highway, fuming, he proceeded to stick out his thumb in an attempt to hitch a ride back home.

My brother and I were wiping the blood from our heads and the tears from our eyes, begging our dad to please not leave us alone with all the "women folk." As we climbed over the seat and back onto our metal platform, we were now catching a glimpse through the bubbles of this "green" man on the other side of the universe.

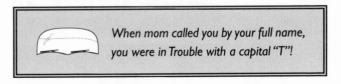

When mom called you by your full name, you were in Trouble with a capital "T"!

My mom put down her maps and journal, climbed into the driver's seat, threw it into reverse and proceeded to back up on the road. Past all of the now curious and unharmed cows. With cars buzzing by, my mom took charge. "Mother, you be quiet! Bill, get back in this car this instant!" She whispered through clenched teeth. (Mom never liked to create a scene in front of the neighbors.) Dad yelled his response from 50 yards away, "I'm not getting in there with that crazy woman!" Grandma had her say, "I don't know what he's so mad about. The cows, the cows will run all over the road!" Back to my mom, "Mother, I don't want to hear another peep from you. Now, William Howard Armstrong, get in this car!" When mom called you by your

full name, you were in Trouble with a capital "T"!
(I learned that lesson the hard way.)

Thankfully, order was somehow restored. My dad
came back, reluctantly. You can only imagine the
stares exchanged in the front row between the
two fighters on the title card. It was like watching
boxers toe-to-toe in the middle of the ring right before blows are exchanged. A good, old fashioned,
stare down at high speed. We somehow managed
to get all the way to the west coast. Alive. And still,
I love to drive! Oh, it should be pointed out that
the trip back home two weeks later was uneventful. We dropped Grandma off with the relatives in
Oregon.

 *We may not have been blessed with
enormous wealth, but there was sure a
lot of joy and laughter in our home.*

I'm so thankful for my childhood. We may not have
been blessed with enormous wealth, but there was
sure a lot of joy and laughter in our home. My dad
taught me a "blue collar" work ethic that sticks
with me today. My mom blessed me with organizational skills, a sense of humor, and the ability to
"make lemonade out of lemons." It's one of her
favorite expressions.

Our trip to Oregon is a perfect example. Not everything went as planned, but the memories of that trip have lingered to this day. It's one of our favorite things to reminisce about at family gatherings. My love for the road and the great adventures it provides may have been born on that maiden voyage to the West.

On the Road Again

It's a good thing that I like to get behind the wheel. My job for the past twenty plus years as an announcer in the Big 12 Conference for men's basketball sort of requires it. From where I live, I can drive to seven of the twelve schools. I generally put more than 12,000 miles on my car each season. Sometimes I'll have a passenger or two, but for the most part, these are solo journeys. I like it either way. It's fun to have someone along for the ride, to keep me company. But it's also good to be alone. Lost in my thoughts, my music, or talk radio. Sometimes I turn everything off, even my cell phone, and just think. It's like meditation at seventy miles an hour. Very relaxing. Soothing even. Balm for the soul.

Over the course of this book, I'll take you on a journey to some of my haunts around the Midwest. I promise to try to be entertaining and maybe even a little thought provoking. It's not too long of a trip. And I won't make you sit in the "way back." You've got a front row seat, riding shotgun. Your seat's heated, or cooled, your choice. You will have your own temperature control and everything. It'll be neat and clean. I like things orderly if that's okay. Nothing but the finest for you. And I'll do my best to make you comfortable.

When I'm out there on the road, all by myself, I sometimes dream about driving in every state. That's sort of a goal of mine. I think at last count I've knocked off 45 of the 50. Alaska and a few New England states in the far Northeast still to go. One of these Septembers, I'd like to do the "fall foliage" trip to Vermont, New Hampshire and the surrounding area. Maybe ESPN will send me up there for a football game, and I'll turn that into a weeklong trip.

Suffice it to say, I'm sort of a "road geek." My Rand McNally Atlas is like a best friend. I haven't yet plunked down the money to get a navigational system installed. Next car, I promise. Love the gadgets. I'm a car salesman's dream. I like all of the options. The creature comforts. And I like it clean. I'm a member of a car wash service, so I have mine cleaned, both inside and out, every time I get gas. Much more about this little peccadillo of my personality later on. I don't want to scare you off before we get too far down the road.

I'm so excited to get on the road with you. To take a little trip. Get away for a few hours. Just head out on the highway and see where this journey takes us. I invite you to buckle up and come along for the ride. I hope you brought some tunes or something interesting to talk about. I love good conversation. That's really what I hope this book feels like. You and I having a great talk on our way to wherever. Gas in the tank? Check. Let's hit the trail.

Chapter Two
The Windshield and the
Rear-View Mirror

For many years, in addition to announcing numerous games for the Big 12 conference, I also served as the "voice" of the Iowa State Cyclones on their own television network. This meant that about fifteen times a year, I would drive up to do a game. I would typically make this a one-day trip. From my home in Kansas City to Hilton Coliseum in Ames, Iowa is about three hours and 45 minutes. Give or take a rest stop or two. So for a seven o'clock game, I will usually leave home at one to make sure I arrive two hours ahead of the opening tip. I always keep a close eye on weather forecasts. You can count on a winter storm at some point during the season. If it looks real bad, I'll leave a day or maybe two early to make sure I don't miss the game. I'm proud to say that in more than twenty years of doing this, I've never missed one.

I've had a few close calls, mind you. Like the time I was living in Tulsa, Oklahoma, and was broadcasting Cyclone basketball. Usually, I didn't drive the whole way. But to save the network some money, I flew from Tulsa to Kansas City, and then drove three and a half hours from the K.C. International airport to Ames. The difference in the travel plans saved the network about $500 per trip. I didn't mind the inconvenience. I knew they were operating on a limited budget.

On this particular day, I got to the airport in Tulsa only to find out it was fogged in. No flights either in or out, and it looked like the fog was there to last all day. So I did the only thing I could do. I got in the car and made the eight-hour drive from Oklahoma to Iowa for the game. I made it, 15 minutes before the opening tip. Whew! Talk about cutting it close.

What is it about Trips to Iowa?

That same winter, while still living in Tulsa, ESPN assigned me to a game in Cedar Rapids, Iowa. It was the Continental Basketball Association All Star game. And for this one there were some real extenuating circumstances. A few days prior to this assignment, I had a scheduled medical procedure. Let's just say I had routine surgery in a delicate area and leave it at that. I was doing pretty well, but I really shouldn't have been traveling. You know what they say though-the show must go on.

I've always taken pride in showing up to do the job. I'm always prepared, on time, and happy to be there. I'm lucky; I love what I do for a living. It's my dream job. I like virtually everything about it.

The preparation. The game itself. Working without a net on a live broadcast. The adrenalin rush that comes with that. I love talking to the coaches, players, media members, fans and the great crews I have the privilege of working with. I even like the travel. Especially when I can drive to a location.

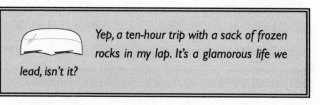

Yep, a ten-hour trip with a sack of frozen rocks in my lap. It's a glamorous life we lead, isn't it?

But let's get back to the trip to Iowa just days after my little procedure. I'm at the airport in Tulsa to fly all the way to Cedar Rapids. Same thing, fog. Again, back in the car. Only this time with a crucial pit stop at the convenience store to get a bag of ice. Yep, a ten-hour trip with a sack of frozen rocks in my lap. It's a glamorous life we lead, isn't it?

When there isn't bad weather or surgical procedures to factor in, most of the trips are pretty routine. I love the drive to Ames. I know that's weird, but I really do. I know the path up I-35 as if I were walking down to the corner store. And I love the people in Iowa. Salt of the earth folks. Great fans, and they love their Cyclones. During broadcasts, we always talk about "Hilton Magic." Some of that magic has sort of disappeared in recent years, but the place is still pretty special. The people are what make that place, and they're great, just great. I've had more folks come up to me after a game and say, "Can't wait to go home and watch the game!" They just saw the game! But they'll tape it and watch it again and again. Now that's what I call a fanatic. God bless them! I should stay and mingle with these folks, but I'm typically headed south on I-35 to my home. Hitting my driveway about one in the morning. Again, glamorous. Again, love it.

The Windshield and The Rear-View Mirror

As I was driving to Ames, Iowa, last winter, I had this thought bombarding my mind. The rear-view mirror is about 1/50th the size of the windshield. Car manufacturers get what we all should get, and that is, it's far more important to look forward than to look back. Think about it. We spend so much of our time in the rear-view mirror that we tend to miss the spectacular show right in front of our eyes. Now make no mistake. Sometimes it's great to look back. Something that just caught our attention and we need another peek. Or someone in the distant past that brings a smile to our face. A warm memory. A great story from long ago. The soundtrack of our life. This is the time when the rear-view mirror serves a great purpose.

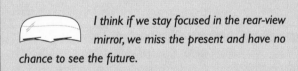

I think if we stay focused in the rear-view mirror, we miss the present and have no chance to see the future.

But let's face it. Most of the time we tend to look back with regret. Of jobs or loves lost. Of decisions made that maybe didn't turn out for the best. I think if we stay focused in the rear-view mirror, we miss the present and have no chance to see the future.

In my work as a sports announcer I am confronted with the principals of the windshield and the rear-view mirror on each broadcast. It's an iron clad rule in television for us to never miss "live action." It's fine for us to glance through the rear-view mirror at an instant replay. In fact, we often look at a previous play from several different camera angles. We're constantly in search of the best view of the past. But we try to never miss something that is happening now. Our view must always be focused on the windshield first. If we get caught looking at a replay when the action is going on we could miss something spectacular. There's no worse feeling than looking at our rear-view mirror while a player is creating another highlight in the windshield. The audience gets cheated and we feel awful.

If you've lived on this earth for any amount of time, you've had disappointments. We all have. It's what we choose to do with these moments that make or break us. We can throw ourselves a giant "pity party." I've been a participant in a few of those. But I've found that if I linger too long at that party, I become pitiful. Now when something unfortunate happens, I allow myself only a certain time frame to wallow around at that gathering. Then I get back in the game. It's a choice of the mind. Trust me, the body will follow. If we can win on the battlefield of the mind, we have a greater chance to live a happier, more fulfilled life.

From my own personal experience, I've discovered that the so called "good times" never last, but neither do the "bad times." It's easy to lose sight of this when we're in the midst of a struggle. For whatever reason, we tend to live a life of waiting for the other shoe to drop. We can't get our eyes off of the rear-view mirror because of the pain we feel.

Memories of a Beloved Brother

I lost my brother in a plane crash twenty years ago. For the longest time, I kept looking back through the rear-view mirror at the event that tragically ended his life.

He was flying cargo for a company in Michigan. He was alone, flying solo. He took off from Memphis late at night and immediately had trouble and had to turn around. He didn't make it back to the airport. Instead, he crashed on a golf course less than a couple of miles from the runway. The impact of the crash was so violent that it hurled his body out of the cockpit and onto the ground. He was killed instantly. My faith, and, more importantly, *his* faith tell me he's in Heaven. Still, this offered me little comfort in the days and even years following this event. I stayed focused in the rear-view mirror. And I stayed focused on that last flight.

My brother loved to fly. He was passionate about it. And he was an excellent pilot. When he was at the very end of his training, I was invited to go with him and his instructor for an exercise they call "touch and go." This is where they practice take-offs and landings. Again and again. No sooner would we be airborne than we would loop around and land. Then, without even stopping, back in the air again. And again. When we finally landed for good, I literally kissed the ground and my lunch good-bye. But what I learned from that excursion was that my brother really loved what he was doing, and he was very skilled at it.

He was only 26 at the time of the crash. He left behind a wife and a 18-month-old daughter. He was loved by everyone. I loved him immensely.

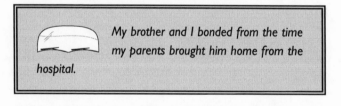
My brother and I bonded from the time my parents brought him home from the hospital.

My brother and I bonded from the time my parents brought him home from the hospital. It was great to have another "man" in the house. I have two older sisters, and I was tired of being outnumbered, and sometimes bullied. My brother came seven years after me. A "mistake" baby. He was no mistake. He was a gift.

My brother would shadow me everywhere I went. I didn't mind. I even welcomed the company. I had a paper route for a few years. *The Detroit News*. It was an afternoon paper. Everyday after school, my brother and I would hop on my Schwinn heavy-duty bike and head out on the route. Both of us on the one bike. It didn't come with gears either. On the days when the paper was thin enough that you could throw it, my brother would ride on the back of the bike. If I missed a porch, and some-times I did on purpose, he would jump off and put the paper in its proper place. Then, after getting it on the porch or wherever, he'd run to catch back up to me. He was a trooper. As a reward, I would usually take him to the corner store on our way home to get a piece of penny candy or something. Talk about child labor. My whole operation would have been shut down if the authorities had known about it.

Back then our television didn't come with a million channels or a remote control. My brother was the remote. If we needed the channel changed, he would "volunteer." He hardly ever complained. A real servant's heart. Great kid, really great.

When I was old enough to date, my brother would often tag along. My dates didn't mind; in fact, I think they liked him more than me.

Even as I write this, I can't adequately describe what it meant for me to have a little brother. I loved him, and he worshiped me. Maybe that's why I loved him. He wasn't perfect, none of us are. But he was special.

Not Getting Stuck in the Rear-View

If you've lost a loved one prematurely, you know what I'm talking about. It took me years to get myself out of the rear-view mirror. Or at least to a healthy view of the past. See, I was focused on the end of his life, and not the whole biography. When I looked back, I only remembered the terrible pain of his death. Not his wonderful life. Plus, I had the misguided thought that if I didn't continue to mourn my brother; people would think I didn't care. Or that I didn't really love him. Obviously not a healthy point of view.

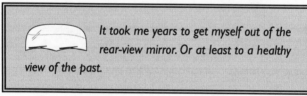

It took me years to get myself out of the rear-view mirror. Or at least to a healthy view of the past.

But that's what happens when we get "stuck" in the rear-view mirror.. Our view gets distorted. Objects appear to be larger than life itself. I think it has that printed right there on the mirror. You get my point. Now when I glance, and it's only a glance, in the rear-view mirror, I think of all the cool things my brother and I did together. Of all the laughs, and that brings a smile to my face, not a frown. I discovered there was nothing I could do to change the past. As much as I wanted to play God and bring him back, it wasn't happening. And I was missing a lot of the road right in front of me.

> *As much as I wanted to play God and bring him back, it wasn't happening. And I was missing a lot of the road right in front of me.*

Closing a Rear-View Chapter

A year ago, I had to fly to Charlotte, North Carolina. I was on my way to Wake Forest for a football game on ESPNU. My plane made a stop in Memphis. At the very airport near where my brother died. Normally I get an aisle seat, but for this flight I was assigned a seat by the window. As we were making our approach into the Memphis airport, I looked down at the ground below. I was staring at the very golf course where my brother crashed! If this had happened while I was still focused in the rear-view mirror, I would have been reduced to a pool of tears in that seat. The popular term these days is "closure." But that moment gave me a chance to say good-bye. Instead of tears in the rear-view, I looked through the windshield of wonderful times together.

The reflections I now see in the rear-view mirror serve as a lesson plan for my life, not the life I'm living in the present.

Time to Refuel—
Pit Stop #1

Time for our first pit stop. This is a chance to reflect on some of the road signs I'd like to point out along the way.

Point of Interest—
The Windshield & The Rear-View

In this chapter we talked about the importance of keeping our focus on the road ahead. It's easy to get caught up in the past, but think for a moment about what we may be missing by not checking out the landscape right in front of our eyes. What lies on the road ahead? What's in the present or near future that looks like a very attractive vista?

Point of Interest—
Don't Get Stuck in the Rear-View

Think also about how easy it is to get "stuck" in the rear-view mirror. What are you hanging onto in your past that needs to be put aside? Or at least put in its proper place? Take some time to reflect on these two points of interest before getting back on the road.

Chapter Three
The Windshield and the Bug

One of my favorite expressions is, some days you're the windshield, and some days you're the bug. Perfect. A friend of mine recently asked "What's the last thing that goes through a bug's mind when it hits the windshield?" "I don't know," I responded. Wryly, he said, "It's feet!"

So are you a bug or a windshield today? Sure it varies, but that's one of the beauties of life. Wouldn't it be boring if every day were the same? Bill Murray wonderfully depicted this in the movie "Groundhog Day." He spends what seems like an eternity living through the same day, Groundhog Day, in tiny but quaint Punxsutawney, Pennsylvania. But what I love is that his character finally figures out what's going on. Instead of wallowing in the rearview mirror, he forges ahead. He gets a fresh view each day from the windshield. He becomes a concert pianist. An artist, an ice sculptor. He wins over the whole town with his up-beat view of life. Ultimately, he wins the girl of his dreams. Ah, only in Hollywood.

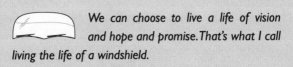

We can choose to live a life of vision and hope and promise. That's what I call living the life of a windshield.

But the principles are the same for us. We could go through life playing out each day like any other. Or we can choose to live a life of vision and hope and promise. That's what I call living the life of a windshield.

Texas Hold 'Em in Osceola

One more quick story about a trip to Iowa State. Last winter I made the journey with one of my best friends in life, Kevin Shank. Kevin is one of the most talented men I have had the privilege of working with in broadcasting. He's a gifted producer and director. He can wear both hats equally well. I've rarely seen him in a bad mood. He's a hard worker, but he likes to have fun, too. Plus, he's paid his dues.

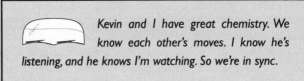

Kevin and I have great chemistry. We know each other's moves. I know he's listening, and he knows I'm watching. So we're in sync.

Kevin started his career as a cameraman. Moved to videotape replays. Then became a technical director, before moving into his present positions of producer or director. I think the experience he gained each step of the way has helped him understand each person's role in a production truck. That makes him a very good and respected leader in his field. On top of all that, he listens very well to what the announcers are saying. That helps him get the shots that make each broadcast the best it can be. Kevin and I have great chemistry. We know each other's moves. I know he's listening, and he knows I'm watching. So we're in sync. Too many times, a director will "cut" a show his way and make the announcer chase him around the broadcast. Or the announcer won't pay attention to what's actually on the screen, and the director is constantly playing catch-up. With Kevin, we are both on the same wave length. I love working with him. He just gets it.

Anyway, we were traveling up I-35 to Ames. Along the way, we decided to stop in Osceola, Iowa. There's a small riverboat casino there. Now, I'm not a gambler. I've always held to the theory that all those big, shiny buildings in Las Vegas weren't built because everyone's winning a lot of money. But I do like to play cards. That's part of being a firefighter's son. All those hours my dad spent, when not fighting fires, in the firehouse playing Gin Rummy. He might not have passed on his fix-it or bravery traits, but I do know how to play cards. Plus, I've seen a few hours of poker on ESPN. With that as my tutorial, we stop at this casino for a little "Texas Hold 'Em."

Dad might not have passed on his fix-it or bravery traits, but I do know how to play cards. Plus, I've seen a few hours of poker on ESPN

Fortunately the stakes were not high. Less than $100 if I remember right. Action was going on for a while when all of a sudden I was dealt two Aces as my hold cards. This is the best starting hand you can possibly have. The next five cards are "community" cards. You make the best hand you can with your two hold cards and the five on the table, using only five total cards. The first three cards came out Ace, ten, Queen. Of different suits. So no possible flush, but I was a little concerned about a straight. Still, I now had three Aces, and felt I had the best hand. I thought I was being coy by "slow-playing" the table. I saw this maneuver on ESPN and it worked out well for the professionals. Three others stayed in and the pot was building. I was already starting to calculate my winnings.

The next card was another ten. Wow! I had a full house, with Aces up! Now, not even a straight could beat me. Again, I "slow-played." Man, I was going to take this table down. The next card was a harmless three. No help to anyone. I proudly went "all in." I was so excited to show my hold cards and display my full house. I was about set to rake the pot when a nice man in overalls proudly displayed his hold cards. Two tens. He had four of a kind. That's when

I thought the title of this book would be, I've got a Full House, but the Rest of the World has Four of a Kind. Kevin and I laughed all the way to Ames, and back home again. That day I was definitely the bug, and the farmer was the windshield. Good for him. He got the winnings, but I got a great story to tell for the rest of my life. The way I look at it we were both winners.

> *I've taken on the philosophy of life that you have great experiences, where everything goes as planned, and that's terrific. But you also have great memories when they don't.*

Welcome to The State of Mind

I've taken on the philosophy of life that you have great experiences, where everything goes as planned, and that's terrific. But you also have great memories when they don't. In fact, I've usually laughed harder at the so-called mistakes than at perfection. A friend was recently planning her daughter's wedding. She is one of the classiest and most organized people in the world. But she was really stressing out over this wedding. She wanted everything to come off without a hitch. She wanted perfection. I could sense her growing anxiety. So I tried to relax her by saying, "Either it goes off perfectly, and that will be great. Or it doesn't, and you'll have a great story to tell." As long as no one is hurt, it's all-good. By the way, the wedding came off without a hitch. I had no doubt.

This woman and her husband sort of "adopted" me when I was in high school. They were a newly married couple and I don't think they could afford a dog, so I became their puppy. They would have been better off with a kennel full of dogs. Sure I was house-trained. But they didn't know I had hollow legs and would eat them out of house and home. They've become life-long friends. I've learned a lot from them through the years. We've shared a lot of laughs and a lot of pizza. They both have so many great qualities.

One of the things they've passed on to me, almost by osmosis, is a great fondness for cleanliness. Not that this trait wasn't taught in my home-it was. But the obsession with keeping things neat and orderly was cemented into my soul by this couple.

Getting a Clear View in Life

I'm a fanatic when it comes to keeping the windows of the car clean. I like a nice clear view. I don't like pet smudges or fingerprints. I even go to the trouble to clean the inside of the windshield to remove all the air conditioner film that collects and distorts the view. I hate to admit this, but I get a bit perplexed when the sun hits the windshield just right and I've discovered that I've missed a spot. Or I notice a new imperfection. Driving at night in the summer creates a mural of dead bugs splattered all over the windshield. The biggest and juiciest ones always seem to splat right in my direct vision. Sometimes I think it's a bug conspiracy. I think they're having secret meetings planning on how to mar my outlook on life.

> *Sometimes I think it's a bug conspiracy. I think they're having secret meetings planning on how to mar my outlook on life.*

In the winter, there's sleet and slush and ice. Let me ask you this, why does your washer fluid always run out at the exact time when you need it most? You're driving along on streets that are melting. The vehicle in front of you is giving you a slushy shower. It starts to freeze and dry on contact. Within minutes, you can hardly see a thing. Just then, no washer fluid. So then you follow real close to get the spray and time the wipers before the sludge dries.

Or how about when ice forms on your wiper blade and only gives you a small, little streak of a clean windshield. That's when we perform the "roll down the window, grab the wiper when it comes up, and give it a smack" maneuver. At 60 miles per hour.

Raise your hand if you've driven in a crouched position trying to see through a tiny little chasm of light at the bottom of the windshield created by the defroster. I see those hands. Me too. That can't be safe, right?! How many of you have tried to scrape ice from your windshield with a key or a credit card because you didn't have an ice-scraper in the car?

When we lived in Colorado, driving in the snow became almost an everyday occurrence. They don't use salt on the streets there like in Kansas or where I learned to drive, Michigan. They use small pebbles to give you traction. It works fine except those little stones get thrown up against the front of your vehicle. It's like following someone who's firing shots at you with a pellet machine gun. By the end of the winter season, your windshield looks like a million tiny little pick axes went to work. Chips and cracks all over the place. They even offer auto insurance to cover the cost of a new windshield each season. Note to self: look into owning a windshield shop in Denver.

So, wait a minute. What are we saying here? It's important to look forward through the windshield of our lives, but then the windshield gets dirty? It becomes marred and disfigured. Sludge and ice and even rocks pelt away at our view. It almost seems like looking through the rear-view mirror gives us a clearer view. Doesn't this seem like a contradiction? No, not really. What's different about this scenario from our ordinary lives? Absolutely nothing.

A Skewed Point of View

That's life. That's reality. Sometimes our view does get skewed. Sometimes outside forces, out of our control, cause our vision to get blurred. People tell us we can't do something, and for whatever reason we believe them. That's blurred vision. That's sleet on the windshield. Or bug juice.

> *Sometimes our view does get skewed. Sometimes outside forces, out of our control, cause our vision to get blurred.*

Through no fault of our own, something horrible happens. Like my brother's death. That's the grime of the road. That happens. You can't prevent it. Well, I suppose you could if you never left the garage. If you never got behind the wheel. If you choose not to live life. If you take the risk of taking that trip of life, sometimes bad things will happen. Even if you have the best of intentions.

Five Downs at Faurot Field

A perfect example of letting outside influences blur our vision happened to me on October 6, 1990. That day I was working for Prime Network. Prime would eventually evolve into what is now Fox Sports Net. But on that chilly October day, I was in Columbia for a football game between 12th ranked Colorado and unranked Missouri. On the surface, this game carried no real significance, but it has since become one of the most famous games in college football history.

> On the surface, this game carried no real significance, but it has since become one of the most famous games in college football history.

The Buffaloes were heavily favored to win this game over the seemingly overmatched Tigers. But everyone forgot to tell the Missouri players and coaches what an underdog they were. Mizzou played great. With less than three minutes to go, the Tigers had the lead 31–27. To compound the situation, the Buffs were playing without their starting quarterback, Darian Hagan. But they weren't using this as an excuse.

The back-up QB, Charles Johnson, started the last gasp drive deep in his own territory. He was able to move his team down the field. With forty seconds left, Johnson hit tight end Jon Boman with a pass. Boman took it down to the two yard line. He might have scored on the play, but he slipped on a slick artificial surface. Players from both teams were slipping on the field all afternoon. Colorado Head Coach Bill McCartney, a Mizzou alum, didn't make many friends back home in Missouri when he complained about this after the game.

Stay with this because this is when the real confusion begins. The catch by Boman gave the Buffaloes a first down at the two yard line. Just six feet from a win. Johnson got his team up to the line of scrimmage and spiked the ball to stop the clock.

Playing in a hurry-up offense, CU then had talented running back Eric Bieniemy run into a pile at the line. He was stopped at the one. Are you keeping track? That's two downs right? Colorado used their last time-out. This is the point where outside influences changed the course of history.

During the time-out my broadcast partner, Dave Lapham, and I started to discuss Colorado's options. We concluded that the Buffs only real strategy was to throw the ball. They had no time-outs remaining, so if a run was stopped short of the end zone, they wouldn't have enough time to run another play.

Well, guess what? After the time-out, Colorado tried to run Bieniemy again. And again he was stopped! Johnson quickly got his team back in formation and "He downed the ball on Fourth Down!" I said on the air with great surprise. There were two seconds left. I was stunned. I thought Colorado had just lost the game by throwing the ball into the turf on the last play. Immediately I was swept into a parallel universe.

You see, after second down, the officials never changed the down marker. The scoreboard never changed the down from second to third. To be honest, I never noticed. I was just counting down the plays in my head. So I thought I nailed it when I yelled, "He downed the ball on fourth down!" My partner, noticing the signs on the field, immediately said, "No, that was third down. What a head's up play by the back-up quarterback."

Again, I was stunned. What did I miss? Sure enough, the down marker and scoreboard both confirmed my partner. So I said, somewhat flustered now, "Okay, here comes fourth down all over again!" That's when the producer gave me an earful. "Dave, come on! Get your head in the game! It's not fourth down again. It's just fourth down. This is crunch time, concentrate!"

 *Boy, did I feel foolish. The biggest play of the game, and everyone was telling me what an idiot I was.*

Boy, did I feel foolish. The biggest play of the game, and everyone was telling me what an idiot I was. As Charles Johnson ran the ball in for a Colorado touchdown on the next play, I was running the previous four plays back in my head. First down-he downed the ball. Second down-Bieniemy run. Third down-Bieniemy run. Fourth down-he downed the ball! Fifth down-touchdown! What did I miss? As it turned out, nothing.

Since everyone and everything was telling me I was wrong, I felt I had no choice but to believe them. I was brainwashed. My partner, my producer, the scoreboard, the down marker on the sideline, the officials. Even the coaches and players from both teams. They all confirmed what looked like the biggest boo-boo I had ever made on a broadcast. I wish I had the courage of my conviction, but I went along with the crowd. I was influenced by outside forces.

This happens in life too doesn't it? We let everyone and everything tell us why we can't do something. We're not gifted enough. We're not talented enough. We didn't have the right background or the right training. We lack this or that.

As I peek through the rear-view mirror, I wish I could have that moment in Columbia back. I wish I had not been brainwashed. I was right. (For a change.) Everyone else was wrong. Now, that doesn't happen very often. But it did that day. It has helped serve as a reminder to not let outside influences hold me back.

 It has helped serve as a reminder to not let outside influences hold me back.

By the way, about fifteen minutes after this play happened, I was vindicated. Officials confirmed that there indeed had been a fifth down. But since the mistake occurred between second and third down, there was nothing they could do at that point to change the ultimate outcome of the game. Colorado won 33–31. Sadly, the referee from that game never officiated another college football game.

The Buffaloes won every game the rest of the way and finished the season at 11–1–1. They beat Notre Dame in the Orange Bowl. They were awarded a share of the National Championship along with Georgia Tech. As an aside, I think it's safe to say the Bowl Championship Series was born out of the confusion of that fifth down game.

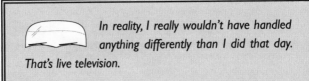

In reality, I really wouldn't have handled anything differently than I did that day. That's live television.

In reality, I really wouldn't have handled anything differently than I did that day. That's live television. A whole stadium of almost 50,000 people was confused. Why should I be any different? One thing is certain; I didn't allow that experience to numb my senses. I didn't allow it to keep me from getting behind the wheel again.

Here's what I know. I can stay in the garage where it's "safe," or I can gas up the car and hit the highways. The choice seems pretty simple. The view never changes in the garage. You spend every day looking at the same four walls. It smells in there. It might be "safe," but it's not much fun.

But if we risk of taking a trip, we expand our view. We can go anywhere we want. We have the chance to see spectacular vistas. Sunsets over the Pacific. The majestic Rocky Mountains. The peaceful sight of cattle grazing on rolling meadows. Rows and rows of corn stretching for acres and acres. Sure, there will be the occasional pothole. It might get stormy. But I've even found pleasure in the storm. The challenge of getting through an obstacle. The joy of the feeling of accomplishment when we get by that roadblock.

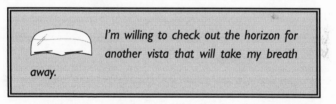

I'm willing to check out the horizon for another vista that will take my breath away.

It's a conscious decision we make. We can stay in the garage or take a trip. It's up to us. Despite a few setbacks. A few accidents, some of them fatal. I've made the decision to stay on the road. See what happens around the next bend. There may be orange cones or red flares, but there might also be the breathtaking sight of waving wheat on a

Kansas farm in the Flint Hills. There's real beauty in life. I'm willing to take the chance of seeing that rainbow over the next hill. I'm willing to check out the horizon for another vista that will take my breath away. It sure beats staring at spare tires and rakes and brooms hanging on the walls of my garage.

Stuck in the Garage

For the past five years, I've sort of been stuck in my garage. Six years ago, my contract expired with the Colorado Rockies. I wasn't re-hired. It was a pretty tough blow. Not only loss of a pretty good income, but also loss of what I thought was my dream job. And in a sense, a certain loss of identity. I took great pride, too much pride really, in being the "voice of the Rockies."

> *I wasn't re-hired. It was a pretty tough blow. Not only loss of a pretty good income, but also loss of what I thought was my dream job. And in a sense, a certain loss of identity.*

Ever since I was a little kid growing up in Detroit, I hoped that one day I would get the chance to broadcast major league baseball. To be honest, I didn't even know what that meant, but I wanted to do it. So first, for three years, with the Kansas City Royals starting in 1993, and then with the Rockies for six years I lived that dream. Nine years of touring major league parks each summer. It was a blast. Better than I imagined it would be.

So when it ended after the 2001 season, I was kind of spinning my tires for a while. No, it was worse, my car was up on the jacks. I still had other work with basketball and football and even collegiate wrestling. But I was missing a big part of my career. My car had taken a hit on the road of life.

For the next five years I applied for every job that opened in baseball. Unfortunately there weren't many opportunities and I always fell just short of landing back in the booth in the "bigs."

The biggest blow came just recently. The Kansas City Royals decided to make a change in who was going to produce their games. They were switching from the Royals Sports Television Network to Fox Sports. It appeared to me that the effect of this decision would lead to a possible change in the television booth. I had hope of getting back with the Royals. Back with my old broadcast partner, former Kansas City pitcher Paul Splittorff. Back with Kevin Shank, who produces the games. Back in a very familiar saddle. All the stars seemed to align. But the ballclub and Fox Sports decided to stay "in house."

 But here's the real key—I didn't stay "by the side of the road."

They switched one of the radio announcers to television and the television announcer over to radio. I'm not arguing with the decision. Both of the chosen broadcasters are friends of mine and excellent at what they do. Still, this was like a flat tire to my career. It was certainly cause to force me to pull over onto the shoulder. But here's the real key—I didn't stay "by the side of the road." I made the necessary repairs and moved on.

A New Horizon

After five years of trying to stay on the same path, it became apparent that I had hit a big detour. There was really no way to go through this wreck or around it. I had to chart a new course. What I've found is this new path is exciting. It's fresh. It's scenery I haven't seen before. It's so exhilarating! I'm so glad I decided to quit looking through the rear-view mirror at a baseball career, and started to look through the windshield at a thrilling route I never even knew was on the map.

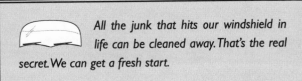

All the junk that hits our windshield in life can be cleaned away. That's the real secret. We can get a fresh start.

One more thing before we hit the rest stop to stretch our legs. All the junk that hits our windshield in life can be cleaned away. That's the real secret.

We can get a fresh start. A little washer fluid, some squeegee action and we're back in business. Another clear view. Even when we take a hit from the inside from fingerprints or air conditioning film, those obstacles can be wiped away. Our windshields come with wipers; so should our lives.

Time to Refuel—
Pit Stop #2

During this pit stop, I want to focus on a couple of different views.

Point of Interest—
The Bug and the Windshield

There are days when it seems as if there if nothing but green lights. Everything is timed out perfectly. There's a flow of traffic that is seamless. Then there are days when it's nothing but red lights. Stopping and starting. A frustrating journey. Sometimes we're just the bug.

But I want us to think about how it's not always that way. Some days the sun does shine. Some days are effortless. And sometimes the only real difference between the two is our own attitude.

Point of Interest—
Don't Let Your View Get Skewed

Let's also think about how we allow outside influences to block the vision of our future. What obstacle is in your way today? What sludge is blocking your view? Why don't we get out the windshield washer and wipe away the dirt from the road? Let's try getting a fresh start today.

Chapter Four
Rest Stop Story Time

Here's a rest stop. A good chance to stretch our legs, get some fresh air. We're in no hurry, so let's grab a bench. Man, it's a beautiful day. Every now and then it's good just to take a break. It's nice to have no real agenda today, isn't it? That's a rare treat. Our lives have gotten so hurried. While the computer and the cell phone have added convenience to our lives, they've also complicated it somewhat.

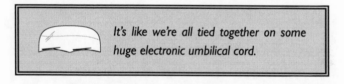

It's like we're all tied together on some huge electronic umbilical cord.

I have a friend in the business that has neither a cell phone nor a computer. We send up smoke signals when we want to reach him. Sometimes it's frustrating, especially when we're traveling together. But he doesn't seem to mind. Meanwhile, the rest of us are constantly checking our e-mails and voice messages and now text messages too. It's like we're all tied together on some huge electronic umbilical cord. It's the price of doing business today; but when we get the chance, it's great to get out of the car and turn off the world for a while.

In the Outfield with George Brett

I told you about getting an opportunity to broadcast for the Kansas City Royals for three years starting in 1993. The year is important because it was George Brett's last. He was putting the finishing touches in what turned out to be a Hall of Fame career. He is at the very top of the list in terms of third basemen in the history of the game of baseball. It was so cool to spend that summer with him. One time they let me shag fly balls during early batting practice. At Tiger Stadium in Detroit no less. Motown. My town.

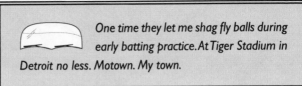

One time they let me shag fly balls during early batting practice. At Tiger Stadium in Detroit no less. Motown. My town.

Growing up in the Motor City was great, especially if you were a baseball fan, which my dad and I were. Still are, for that matter. I remember the first time he took me to a game at the corner of Michigan and Trumball. The ballpark was so huge. Tiger Stadium would seat about 55,000 fans when it was sold out. The lights towering above the neighborhood. The excitement building from the time you saw them sparkling from a few miles away.

I remember my dad parking at the Catholic church near the stadium. The nuns actually took your money and told you where to park. Buying fresh, hot roasted peanuts from a vendor outside. A scorecard, my dad always kept score. Sitting in the stands on a warm summer's night keeping score the way my dad taught me, that's one of the things I cherish to this day. Going through the turnstiles, with the smell of hot dogs, popcorn and cigar smoke wafting through the air. Walking hand in hand with my dad through the concourse, past the concession and souvenir stands, through the tunnel, up a ramp, and there it was. Three decks of baseball history right before my eyes. And what seemed like acres and acres of the greenest, most lush, grass I had ever seen. The centerfield bleachers, the dugouts, the bullpens down each foul line. Plus all the Tiger players in their white uniforms with the distinctive "D" on their chest. Their names displayed along with their numbers on the back. Number 6 Al Kaline, number 25 Norm Cash, number 14 Jim Bunning, number 7 Rocky Colavito, number 3 Dick McAuliffe, just to name a few. I had heard these names on the radio. I had all of their baseball cards. But I had never actually seen them in person before. It was almost more than a kid could handle. My senses bombarded me with a cacophony of sights and sounds and smells. It was like heaven on earth.

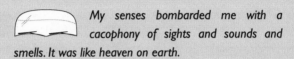

My senses bombarded me with a cacophony of sights and sounds and smells. It was like heaven on earth.

So now, flash forward about 40 years. I'm standing there in right field next to George Brett. He's five feet from me and we're shagging flies! At Tiger Stadium! They could have buried me right there. The thrill of a lifetime. I'm standing there, and this is a little embarrassing to admit, but I was getting emotional. Normal humans like us don't get a chance to do something like that every day. Like never. The memories of all those games I attended in this almost-sacred place came flooding in. The times my dad would take me from my Little League game, in uniform, to see my beloved Tigers play. The Sunday or twi-night doubleheaders. Two games for the price of one.

I was never this close to the field, let alone standing on it. George looks over and sees tears welling up in my eyes. He says, "Army, you okay?" Now I was so embarrassed-I really wanted to be buried right there. Somehow I was able to stammer out, "George, I know this is weird to see a guy out here getting emotional just shagging flies. But I can't help it. This is where I grew up. This is my hometown. I've been to countless games in this place. Usually sitting way out there. (Pointing now at the center field bleachers.) But right now, I'm here with you in right field. Standing in the very spot where my boy-hood idol, Al Kaline, stood." (Mr. Kaline is another Hall of Famer.) Instead of ribbing me-and I'll always love him for this-George got real excited and said, "Yeah! And Ty Cobb stood here, and Babe Ruth! Wow! Army, now you've got me a little choked up. I'm getting goose bumps!" Can you believe that? George Brett is not just a Hall of Fame player. He's a Hall of Fame guy, too.

George Brett's Last Game

The season went on. George didn't have a great year. Certainly not by his illustrious standards. He won three batting titles in his career. One each in the 70s, 80s, and 90s. No one had ever won bat-ting titles in three different decades before. He had more that 3,000 career hits. He probably had more "clutch" hits than anyone else I know. When the game was on the line, if you were a Royals fan, you wanted George Brett at the plate. And he de-livered more times than not.

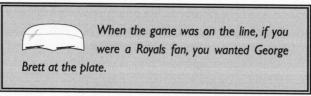

When the game was on the line, if you were a Royals fan, you wanted George Brett at the plate.

The last game of the season was played in Arlington at old Texas Stadium. It was to be the last game ever played in that place. The next year the Rangers moved into their new Ballpark in Arlington. It was also going to be Nolan Ryan's last game for Texas. Ryan threw a record seven no-hitters in his Hall of Fame career. George and Nolan exchanged line-up cards before the game at home plate. Even though both teams were out of any play-off hopes, the mood at the ballpark that day was festive.

Every time George came to the plate, you wondered would this be his last home run. His last double in the gap. When asked what he would like to do with his last at bat, George said he would like to hit a routine ground ball to second base. Then run hard to first just to show the kids how the game should be played. Class. For the record, George singled in his last at bat. I can prove it. I kept the scorecard.

In the third inning of this game, one of our cameras spotted the very familiar figure of Rush Limbaugh sitting behind the Royals dugout. Before Rush became a nationally syndicated conservative talk show host, he worked for the Royals in their public relations department. Rush and George became great friends. In fact, I think they stood up for each other at their respective weddings. We quickly sent someone down to where Rush was sitting and asked if he'd like to regale us with George Brett stories. He agreed. So for about three innings, Rush Limbaugh put politics off to the side and talked about his friend. It was compelling and quite riveting. After a bit, I wondered if Rush might like to do a little play-by-play of the game. He said, "Are you kidding? That's always been a dream of mine!"

Let me set the scene. The Rangers were batting and the Royals had a pitcher named Hipolito Pichardo on the mound. Manuel Lee, a light-hitting shortstop, was up to bat for Texas. Rush's call went something like this. "Here's the pitch from Pichardo. It's a slider and Lee gets his bat on it and hits a soft fly down the line in right. No one's gonna catch that. Hey, they're not even going for the ball!" Well, the umpire had signaled a foul ball. I didn't want to embarrass Rush, but I had to get the truth out there. Almost in a whisper I said, "Rush, it's a foul ball." If you have ever heard Mr. Limbaugh on the radio, you know he's never wrong. At least in his mind. So he says, "No, that's a fair ball and for some inexplicable reason, no one is going to get it." Now my broadcast partner, Paul Splittorff, got involved. "Well, Rush, the umpire has called it foul." Rush was indignant. "Well, the umpire is wrong!" I have to admit, it was close to being fair. In fact, there might have even been a puff of chalk come up when the ball landed. And the crowd at Texas Stadium was really letting the umps have it. Rush ranted on, "Listen to the crowd, they agree with me, that should be a fair ball." About this time, Rangers manager Kevin Kennedy came out to argue the call. Rush spotted him and said, "See, the manager of the Rangers, he agrees with me too-that's a fair ball." That's when I entered politics into the discussion. I said, "Rush, that might be the first time a Kennedy has ever agreed with you about anything!" "Good line," he said as he exited the booth. Never to be heard from again, at least not on the Royals Television Network.

No need for a pit stop here so let's get back on the road. Who knows, Rush might be ranting on the radio.

Chapter Five
Driving Defensively

This is another great day to travel. Perfect weather, great company, and very little traffic. I'm not a big fan of congested conditions on the road. But then again, who is? We've all been in bumper-to-bumper situations. Wall-to-wall cars and trucks and vehicles of all sorts filling the highway like sardines in a can. Ugh, it gives me the shivers just to think about it. I promise not to dwell in this traffic jam of the mind too long. After all, we were getting along so well. Lost in thoughts of the green pastures of the outfield grass at Tiger Stadium. Memories of the Rockies and the Flint Hills. Cornfields and waving wheat. We'll return to those idyllic places soon, but first I want to share a thought or two about the congestion of our mind.

Driving Defensively

I've always been taught to drive defensively. You know, look out for the other guy. This is especially helpful when it comes to driving in adverse conditions. It's times like these that seem to reveal the worst character in others on the road. There's even a term for it now-road rage. Those angry drivers that come close to wreaking havoc on the highway, and often do. Traffic jams, I think, offer a great metaphor for life.

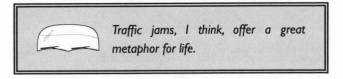

Traffic jams, I think, offer a great metaphor for life.

Anytime the road becomes a virtual parking lot, a whole slew of personalities come to the surface. We've already mentioned the angry driver. The one who always seems to be in a bigger hurry than everyone else. The selfish one who feels that somehow there's a conspiracy and everyone else is out to get him. There's the timid driver. The person who would just as soon pull over and wait this whole thing out. Sit in the rest stop until things clear up. There's Mr. Passive-Aggressive. Okay as long as you don't cut him off, then look out. Everyone's personality traits are worn on their sleeves.

We would all like to go through life without any rush hour traffic. We'd all like the road just to ourselves. Traffic hits us all pretty much the same. No one, except maybe the President, gets his or her own lane. No one gets a free pass.

I think it's important to look out for the other guy in life too. There are times when you can get run over if you don't. There's nothing wrong with getting defensive every now and then.

The more familiar I am with the nuances of each player, the easier it is to broadcast a game.

Basketball Practice with Bob Knight

I have the privilege of watching basketball practice at several different college campuses across the land. It goes with the territory of being a sportscaster. When schedules allow, I like to get in a day before the game itself. This way I can observe the teams. Get familiar with the players, talk to the coaches. It really helps in the preparation. The more familiar I am with the nuances of each player, the easier it is to broadcast a game. If I can learn their faces or body types, and not just their number, I have a much better chance to bring out other aspects of the game. I don't have to concentrate so hard just to get their name right. I can pay even more attention to what they are doing, or trying to do, on the court.

One of the best, if not the best, in teaching defensive principles is Bob Knight of the Texas Tech Red Raiders.

Everyone likes offense, but I love to watch coaches teach defense. One of the best, if not the best, in teaching defensive principles is Bob Knight of the Texas Tech Red Raiders. You may know him as "Bobby" or "The General," but I've been told he prefers "Bob." Out of respect, I still call him Coach Knight, or Mr. Knight. I'm sure I always will.

Coach Knight has won more games than any coach in men's college basketball history. He has won three national championships and a Gold Medal at the 1984 Olympics. He's in a league of his own when it comes to coaching greatness.

I know there are some who have an entirely different opinion of Coach Knight. Timid he's not. He can rub people the wrong way. And sometimes, truthfully, he's played the part of the bully. But even his detractors would have to agree, the guy can flat-out coach.

He demands perfection from his players. He doesn't always get it, but that doesn't stop him from demanding it. One of his famous sayings is, "Most people have the will to win, but few have the will to prepare to win." Big difference. Nowhere is that will more tested than on defense.

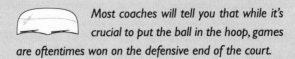

Most coaches will tell you that while it's crucial to put the ball in the hoop, games are oftentimes won on the defensive end of the court.

You don't have to motivate most players to play offense. Most really like the ball in their hands. Most like to score. They like to fill up the stat page with big numbers. It's where you get noticed. Most coaches will tell you that while it's crucial to put the ball in the hoop, games are oftentimes won on the defensive end of the court.

Know Your Options

So driving defensively in life is certainly no negative. Far from it. It's where you can win the game. It's just checking the mirrors to see where the escape routes are just in case the guy in front of you happens to veer into your lane unexpectedly. I think it's important for us to have an alternate plan. To be able to change course in an instant. But, notice, we don't do that without knowing what's there first. And when I say checking the mirrors, I mean just that. Not lingering in the rear-view, just a glance to see our options.

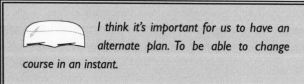 *I think it's important for us to have an alternate plan. To be able to change course in an instant.*

Oftentimes, especially in heavier traffic, I'll think to myself what I would do if something sudden happened. What are my options? Can I get in another lane to avoid an accident?

I remember in Little League, our coaches would tell us to think about what we would do if the ball were hit to us. Before it was hit to us. I've asked numerous major league players, some of them gold glovers, if they follow this practice. To a man, they all do. That's being defensive. But it also makes it possible for you to make the spectacular play. To the un-suspecting eye, it looks like you did it without even thinking. Instinct. Sure, some of that comes into play. Some in athletics, and in life, are just blessed with more ability than the rest of us. That just means the rest of us have to work a little harder.

Driving Defensively is Hard Work But Rewarding

Recently on the television show *60 Minutes*, actor Will Smith was profiled. During the interview he was asked about the secret to his mass appeal. He re-plied, "I don't have the most talent in Hollywood. But I have an insane work ethic. When others are eating, I'm working. When others are sleeping, I'm working." That's my definition of driving defen-sively. It's the desire to do everything possible to make sure you have the best chance to succeed. To leave no stone unturned. It's the will to prepare to win.

Catching on with Steve Largent

After he retired from the National Football League, Steve Largent moved from Seattle to Tulsa. Steve set many records as a wide receiver for the Se-ahawks in a brilliant pro career. His accomplish-ments would eventually lead to a Hall of Fame induction. He will go down in history as one of the greatest receivers in NFL history.

Before going on to professional football, Steve played college ball for the University of Tulsa. So the move back to Oklahoma, his home state, was only natural when he hung it up.

We became friends through various acquaintances. Our friendship blossomed on the tennis court. At first, since I played the sport in college, I was ahead of Steve. But with his superior athletic ability, it didn't take long for him to equal and then eventually surpass me. It was a reminder of cream rising to the top. It also taught me the lesson of hard work helping someone achieve his goals.

When Steve left Tulsa, he was originally drafted by the Houston Oilers. He didn't make it out of training camp. He was cut by their coach, Bum Phillips. Largent had the car packed ready to start a career in criminal justice when Seattle called to offer him a try-out with the Seahawks. The rest, as they say, is history. But Steve worked for it.

Several weeks before training camp even began each year, Steve would start honing his skills. He'd have friends come over to his backyard where he had set up a machine that would fire footballs at blazing speeds. They would shoot the balls at Steve from various distances. Sometimes as close as ten feet. Or they would aim the machine toward the ground, and Steve would dive for the balls on the turf. Again and again. These practice sessions would go on until Steve's hands would get bloody. He explained that he had to "toughen them up" before camp. I don't think anyone ever outworked Steve Largent.

Even late in his career, with his legacy already established, he worked very hard. In his last year, he was injured and had to miss a few games. He was supposed to be out longer, but he worked twice as hard at rehabbing to get back on the field. Whatever the trainers prescribed for him, Steve doubled the workout. That's the kind of determination that helped put him in the Hall. That and a bunch of talent of course.

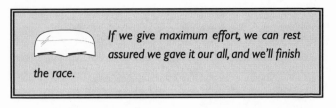

If we give maximum effort, we can rest assured we gave it our all, and we'll finish the race.

Now, it doesn't mean if you work hard, you are guaranteed success, but the chances increase. We shouldn't worry about someone getting ahead who doesn't seem to work as hard we do. We don't control outcomes; we can only control our own effort. We don't drive the other guy's car. He may be behind the wheel of a high-performance machine. But we're all heading in the same direction. If we give maximum effort, we can rest assured we gave it our all, and we'll finish the race. So even if it doesn't work out in our favor, we can relax in the knowledge that we did all we could.

Larry Walker vs. John Vander Wal

I see this played out all the time in athletics. Sometimes you see a guy give everything he has, and yet it's still not enough. I remember once criticizing one of the Rockies players on the air.

The Rockies had one of the best right fielders in the National League when I was there. His name is Larry Walker. He won the Most Valuable Player award in 1997. He won seven Gold Gloves for fielding excellence in his career. He was big and fast and graceful. The best description I ever heard of Larry was from Clint Hurdle. He was the hitting coach at the time; now he's the manager. He said, "Larry chews up yardage in the outfield like a panther on the prowl." And he did.

On this particular day in Cincinnati, Larry was getting the day off. Subbing for him in right field was John Vander Wal. John was an extremely gifted hitter. Especially as a pinch hitter. In fact, he set a record for most pinch hits in 1995. In the third inning of this game a shallow fly was hit toward right. John came running in and had the ball hit the tip of his glove and then fall to the ground for a single. I said on the broadcast, "Oh so close! That's a play Larry Walker would have made." That was totally unfair to John. Larry might have been the only player in baseball who could have made that catch. I apologized to John for the comment. It taught me a lesson in the expectations we place on athletes.

> *I've tended to gravitate to those who have gotten the most out of their talents. Not always the biggest star on the team, but the athlete who succeeded by a sheer will of force.*

Sometimes you see someone maybe a little more "naturally" gifted succeed with seemingly little effort while others are left spinning their wheels. I've tended to gravitate to those who have gotten the most out of their talents. Not always the biggest star on the team, but the athlete who succeeded by a sheer will of force. I think I gravitate to these types because I feel it resonates with my own broadcast career.

When Indiana Basketball Coach Kelvin Sampson was at Oklahoma, he told me. "Dave, when your most talented player is also your hardest worker, you can't lose." Talent and hard work are an unbeatable combination. Just ask the guys on the PGA Tour as they try to compete with Tiger Woods.

Playing the Role of the Underdog

I was the underdog. The guy who came from a background not typically associated with broadcast success. But from the time I was 7 or 8, I wanted to be the guy behind the microphone. I grew up listening to Ernie Harwell describe all the action from Tiger Stadium. Many summer nights were spent at my kitchen table, with my handmade scorecard, keeping up with the Detroit nine on the radio.

> *Many summer nights were spent at my kitchen table, with my handmade scorecard, keeping up with the Detroit nine on the radio..*

I listened to Budd Lynch from the Olympiad calling Red Wings hockey. Van Patrick doing the play-by-play of Lions football. As much as the players themselves, these men of the mic were my heroes.

I didn't make it to the booth because of any great athletic ability. Mr. Harwell described me perfectly in his poem about sportscasters. He writes, "As a kid shortstop, he couldn't stop a grapefruit from rolling uphill, but he can tell a million listeners that Alan Trammel should have played the last guy three steps to the left."

No, I didn't "make it" because of my athletic ability, my background, or by the right genes. That's no knock on my dad, but he didn't pave the way for me to get there. He wasn't a broadcaster-he was a firefighter. A real hero and I am very proud of him. There are many guys now in the booth who were groomed for the job by a father who was an announcer himself. I certainly don't resent those who got a head start this way. They're all very talented broadcasters. They deserve to be there. They've worked hard, too. It's just that their background made it a bit easier to begin the trek. But that's okay. I've certainly enjoyed my journey and wouldn't trade places.

Getting Started...Coffeyville and the Alarm Clock

I was the first in our family to go to college. After four years of studying broadcasting and getting my degree, I still wasn't quite ready for the "real world." After spending all of spring break my senior year looking for a job in broadcasting, and then another few weeks after I got my diploma, it looked like getting started wasn't going to be a cinch.

My first job after college actually wasn't in broadcasting. It was, and you're not going to believe this, working at the Ford Glass Plant in Tulsa, Oklahoma. The part you're really not going to believe, but it's the absolute truth, is that my job was to pull windshields from the assembly line. That's right, windshields! Talk about coming full circle. Now I'm writing a book about windshields and rear-view mirrors. Come to think of it, I wish I could have hauled rear-view mirrors off that line; windshields get pretty heavy after a few hours. Plus, they start to cut through the four layers of gloves and pads you wear to protect your palms. Fortunately I was only there for a month, and then I got my big "break."

> *I had to take a pretty severe pay cut for my first job behind the microphone, but the money didn't matter, this was my dream.*

I had to take a pretty severe pay cut for my first job behind the microphone, but the money didn't matter, this was my dream. After no deliberation, despite making half as much as working on the line at the Glass Plant, I accepted a position at KGGF radio in Coffeyville, Kansas. Now this is a long, long way from the big leagues, but I didn't care. It was a start. Unfortunately, I wasn't ready.

These were professionals I was working with, and my only experience was at the campus radio station. A station that had 10 watts of power. Think about that for a second. Your average light bulb has 60 or 75 watts. We had 10. The signal didn't leave the studio. The only way to hear us was if you brought your transistor radio to the station itself. Some training ground.

> *I worked hard, very hard, but it just wasn't happening. It seemed like the harder I tried, the worse it got. It was like being in quicksand.*

So when I got to Coffeyville, even though I had big aspirations, I had limited skills. I could never get comfortable. I felt intimidated by the older, better and wiser broadcasters I was with. I was used to being the "star" in college, and now I was "Joe College" to these guys. They were nice enough, but I could tell they were growing impatient with my mistakes. I worked hard, very hard, but it just wasn't happening. It seemed like the harder I tried, the worse it got. It was like being in quicksand.

As part of our newscast, we gave funeral arrangements on the air. I would read the announcement of Mrs. So-and-So's dying and her body would be laid to rest at Such-and-Such Cemetery. Our receptionist would take the information and put in on a little slip of paper with all the details. Including the funeral home handling the arrangements. Most of them were from the Coffeyville Funeral home, but every now and then we'd get one from somewhere else.

I got one that was abbreviated; "Funeral arrangements made by the Indy Funeral home." Naturally, I proudly transcribed this to the Indianapolis Funeral home. I wasn't so proud when they told me it was Independence, Kansas, a town about twenty miles away. I'd never heard of it before, but I've never forgotten it since.

Or there was the time I had to read the farm report in the morning. You know, prices of wheat and corn and hogs and such. I got into trouble when I pronounced the report for lambs and ewes as "lambs and ee-wee's." I grew up in the city; I'd never seen the word "ewe" in print before. Some farmer called to inform me that it was "lambs and ewes, you dumb city slicker." Suffice it to say, my career was not off to a flying start.

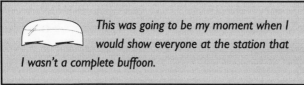

This was going to be my moment when I would show everyone at the station that I wasn't a complete buffoon.

After about a month of this, I was looking for some way to climb out of this hole I had dug. I was given my chance when I was asked to "sign-on" the station that coming Sunday morning. In small towns like Coffeyville, radio stations routinely go off the air at sundown, and then power back up the next day at sunrise. This was going to be my moment when I would show everyone at the station that I wasn't a complete buffoon.

It was a somewhat complicated procedure. There were about 15 or 20 buttons to push to get the power on and the transmitter up and running. I was going to do everything possible to hit this assignment out of the park. The Saturday night before what has become known in Coffeyville as the "day that will live in infamy," I decided to go to bed very early so I would be wide awake. I set the alarm for 4 AM. A full two hours before we were scheduled to come on the air. I double-checked the alarm.

I turned in around 8 PM and tried to get some sleep. But I couldn't sleep. Not with all that I had on my plate. This was my moment of redemption. This was my chance to prove that the last four years studying broadcasting in college wasn't a waste of time. This was my chance to become a professional.

A couple of problems. First of all, it doesn't get dark in Kansas in the summer until around 9:30. Secondly, I had too much on my mind. Thoughts of getting the "sign-on" procedure just right. Now, I had gone over every detail with the station's engineer until he was about ready to strangle me. I wrote it all down. I studied it. I memorized it. I even practiced it when no one was looking. I was about as ready as a rookie could be. But still, I was unsettled. I couldn't calm my mind. I just couldn't sleep.

The year was 1976, and I had one of those "new" digital clock radios. This was cutting-edge technology for the time. Instead of a round face clock, mine had numbers on flip cards that would signal the passing of time. I lay there listening to the minutes pass by. Yes, listening. Those flip cards made a racket, although I had never noticed until that night. Finally sometime about 3 in the morning, I nodded off to sleep.

About 6:30 AM, a full half-hour after we were supposed to be on the air, I got a call from the station manager. He had been jostled out of bed by angry listeners who had called him, wondering why the station wasn't on the air. "Where's Billy Graham and the Hour of Decision?" They would scream into the phone. Following the chain of command, with everything flowing downhill to me, I got the call. "Armstrong, where in the blazes are you, and why aren't we on the air?" I was still trying to grasp where I was, let alone who this guy was screaming at me at such an unseemly hour. It was all starting to come to me in a flash. My month long "career" in broadcasting was over. I'd never work again.

He was kind enough not to fire me that instant, but I knew that day was right around the corner. He screamed, "Get over there and get us up and running! NOW!" I scrambled for my clothes and keys, made the quick drive to the station, and started the "sign on" procedure. Only now, I was so flustered, I couldn't remember the proper sequence. So I had to wake the engineer to help me. You can only imagine his level of enthusiasm.

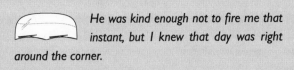

He was kind enough not to fire me that instant, but I knew that day was right around the corner.

While fielding calls from some of the angriest elderly ladies I had ever heard, I finally got us on the air. About 8 AM. Two hours late. Better late than never, they say, but I wasn't so sure.

Here comes the kicker. The next day I was summoned into the station manager's office. The owner was in there too. I had never met him before, and for some reason, he didn't seem so pleasant. The station manager started this inquisition with, "Dave, before we fire you, we'd really like to know how you could foul up this assignment. You had to know you were already living on borrowed time. How? I mean how?" I hesitated for a moment. My parents always told me to tell the truth even if it hurt. "The truth will set you free," they would remind me. Oh, I was going to be set free all right. I just didn't think the truth was going to do it. There were two angry men in the room who were ready to do the honor. "Gentlemen, I think we should just part company. I'm too embarrassed to tell you what happened." I said. They insisted, "No, we'd really like an explanation." Sheepishly, I responded, "Well, I have one of those 'new-fangled' digital clock radios..." At this point, the station manager interrupted. "Oh, I see where this is headed. You set the alarm to wake up to PM instead of AM." "No," I said, "I got the AM part right. My mistake was that I set the alarm to wake up to the radio, and the station was set on our frequency." (I'll give you a moment to let this sink in.) Yes, at 4 AM my alarm came on, playing KGGF, only we weren't on the air.

The two of them sat there, stunned. Dumbfounded. Finally, after what seemed like at eternity. One of them, and I can't remember which one, said, "Well we can't fire you now you're too stupid to make it out there!" Quite a start. Look out, World, I was on my way.

Time to Refuel—
Pit Stop #3

Point of Interest—
It's Important to Have An Alternate Plan...Know Your Options

If life never changed, we would never need to have a map. We'd never have to look for an alternate path. But how much fun would that be? We'd be like Jim Carrey in the movie *"Truman,"* where his character is basically a puppet on a string. Our lives are filled with change. Think for a second about how your life has changed in the past five years. What does it look like for the next five years?

As we look through the windshield at the road ahead, it's good for us to have a couple of different routes in mind. It's good for us to know our options in case one path is blocked. What's your backup plan? Let's get the maps out and chart a new, exciting course.

Chapter Six
The Car Wash

How are you doing? Can I get you anything? You want to play some tunes or something? I like most types of music. From smooth jazz to oldies. Rock and Roll to country. But I'm not a huge Hip-Hop fan. I'm more old school. Remember, I'm from Motown. Stevie Wonder, Diana Ross and the Supremes. The Temptations or the Commodores. I like Smokey Robinson, with or without the Miracles. Gladys Knight and the Pips, Martha Reeves and the Vandellas. So whatever you want to pop in the CD player, it's fine with me. Smooth jazz? Good choice, a little background music to mellow out the day.

I told you earlier about my little obsession with keeping my car clean. I have a friend who is just the opposite. We'll remain friends as long as I don't have to ride in his car anymore. He's a colleague of mine, and we travel extensively together around the Big 12 Conference. I don't want to say anymore, I'm trying my best to protect his identity. I can't tell you his name, but his initials are Reid Gettys.

Reid's Big Green Beast

Last year we were working together in Austin, Texas for a game between the Longhorns and the Oklahoma State Cowboys. Since he lives in Texas, he drove his own car to the Erwin Center where the contest was being held. I flew in from Kansas City, as per normal; I rented a car and met him at the arena for practice.

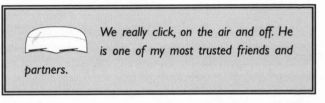

We really click, on the air and off. He is one of my most trusted friends and partners.

Before I go any farther, you should know that I absolutely love working with Reid. He's a play-by-play announcer's dream partner. He knows the game. He played the game. He averaged better than ten assists per game, passing to the likes of Clyde Drexler and Hakeem Abdul Olajuwon with the Houston Cougars. A team that went to three straight Final Four's. Losing in the championship game in both 1983 and '84. They were known as Phi Slamma Jamma. I always kid Reid that he was the Phi part of that equation. He's also coached the game and is very insightful. He does his homework and is a blast to be around. We have chemistry together on the air that isn't always easy to find. We really click, on the air and off. He is one of my most trusted friends and partners. Our friendship spills over to the broadcast, which I think makes for a more enjoyable listen for the audience.

Having said all that, his car, his own personal car is a moving violation. Neither Colombo from the detective series nor Oscar Madison from the *Odd Couple* would get behind the wheel of this mobile pigsty. I didn't know any of this until after practice that day. We have worked together for several years, but I had never been in his private vehicle before. He offered me a ride back to the hotel after the workouts. It seemed like a pretty normal thing at the time. I had no reason to be dubious. After all, on the surface, this guy gives you no cause to believe he lives this dual life in his car. Neat, well-dressed, respected lawyer, broadcaster, husband and father of three by day. Total slob behind the wheel. I had no reason to refuse his offer, so I gladly accepted. What was I thinking? What a disaster!

We walk up to this "thing" in the parking lot. I should have run for the hills of Texas right then. It smelled fishy. It's not that it was suspicious; no, it literally smelled fishy. I would later discover this was from some half-eaten fish sandwich wedged in-between the back seats of this beast. Still, I forged ahead. I tried to open the passenger door, but it was stuck. Figures. He had to come over to my side to help me pry it open.

I've asked myself a million times why I kept heading into this dark hole of filthiness, but I did. I held my nose and proceeded to creep my way in. Being careful in the process to not actually touch anything with my own skin. No telling what diseases were lurking inside this rathole. His vehicle is an old, beat-up, GMC Suburban. So it's safe to say he has been driving this virus center for a while. I think it came with all the options, including an oxygen mask and a tetanus shot for its passengers.

Now I have nothing at all against old. I have nothing at all against someone driving a car or truck for many, many years. My only point is you can get it washed every now and then. Even pigs take baths.

I finally wiggle my way carefully inside. Pulling my sleeve over my hand to grab the handle to wedge that steel trap door shut again. Now I was locked in this death trap. Seated in the fetal position, I instinctively scoped out my surroundings. Much like a soldier would do on recon.

In the center console was a half-eaten apple and an empty plastic, mold-producing, yogurt container with a stainless steel spoon nearby. He tried to explain something about having to "eat on the run." Yes, but half of that meal was still walking around in there.

Fortunately, the trip to the hotel was only a couple of miles, or I might have contracted a disease for which there is no cure. We remain friends, but we'll never ride in his car together again.

Oh, I almost forgot to tell you. His wife was horrified at the thought of my forced kidnapping in his green beast. This year when he came to a game we were doing at Baylor University in Waco, he drove his son's car just in case I might need a ride. Now, while that's very considerate, it proves my point about his own vehicle. When your son's car is cleaner than your own, you might have some issues.

Traveling with a Germ-a-Phobe

I warned you earlier that I was going to tell you about my cleanliness obsession. The older I get, the worse the obsession seems. I find myself becoming more and more of a germ-a-phobic. I don't think it's to the critical stage. After all, I still risk traveling. But I take a lot more precautions. I'm always chewing gummy lozenges that are supposed to prevent a virus when boarding planes. I avoid shaking hands because I don't want to spread disease. I'm more into the "fist-rap" these days. Less contact, I figure.

Public restrooms are my biggest fear. I'm so glad God made me a man. If I were a woman, where I'd be required to sit down all the time, I'd probably have more bladder problems than a urologist's waiting room. I only sit in a public restroom now if it's a medical emergency. But even a "normal" visit presents a problem for a guy like me.

I think it should be a federal law that all public restrooms come with paper towels. Paper towels from automatic dispensers. I don't like the kind where you have to push a lever to get the towel to come out. Why? Because if I get done washing my hands thoroughly and then look over to see that I've got to touch this bar to dispense the paper, it's all over. It's the same bar that hundreds of other guys have touched. So I dispense the paper, and then wash my hands again before grabbing the towel. Sometimes, someone will walk over and rip off the paper I've dispensed, and I've got to start the whole process all over again. It's not always easy being me.

In a perfect world, I can wash my hands, get the paper from the automatic dispenser and then use that paper to grab the door handle on the way out.

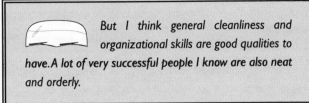

But I think general cleanliness and organizational skills are good qualities to have. A lot of very successful people I know are also neat and orderly.

On the surface, you might think the air dryers for your hands are a more sanitary way to handle the situation. But the problem lies with opening the door after you are done. If it's a door that swings out, no problem. You can open that with your shoulder. But if the door opens in, you have to grab the handle without the use of a paper towel. I don't know where that door handle has been, and I don't want to know. Usually I'll wait for someone to either enter or exit the restroom and then keep the door open with my foot on the way out. I've stood in there waiting for as long as five minutes. I could use toilet paper, but then I'd have to enter the stall. I sure don't want to go in there without a medivac suit. So I wait.

Cleanliness and Organization

What's the point of all this paranoia? I've taken cleanliness and germ-a-phobia to the edge, and sometimes over. But I think general cleanliness and organizational skills are good qualities to have. A lot of very successful people I know are also neat and orderly.

Sure, they may have compartmentalized that quality. Like my friend Reid with the caustic car. Even though his vehicle might be a bit sketchy (and I'm being kind there), his professional life is very organized. His notes for a game are meticulous; his preparation, flawless.

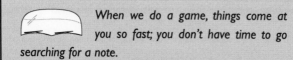

When we do a game, things come at you so fast; you don't have time to go searching for a note.

When we do a game, things come at you so fast; you don't have time to go searching for a note. It had better be right at your fingertip, or the moment will pass. Neatness counts. If you scribble your notes so even you can't read them, then they're useless. If my homework isn't organized in a way that gets me the information that I need when I need it, then it's a waste of paper and ink.

My "spot sheets" are color-coded and neat. The ones I use for football are even laminated after I get done adding all my notes. The reason I laminate them is sometimes you run into inclement weather or a spilled drink, and that can turn your notes into a non-legible mess. My basketball "spot sheets" are taped to the monitor in front of me for easy access. I don't have to look down for a statistic or note-it's right there. If I had clutter all over and was constantly searching for a little tidbit of information, I wouldn't be able to stay focused on the task at hand, the game itself.

I realize I may need to see someone about my cleanliness craze. But it is a mania that has served me well in my career.

Oh, hey, look, there's a spot up ahead to get something to eat. I sure hope they have automatic paper dispensers, or this could take awhile.

Time to Reflect—
Pit Stop #4

This pit stop is more like a car wash. Because in this chapter we talked about cleanliness.

Point of Interest—
Cleanliness is Next to...
Organization!

As we chart our course, let's think about what obstacles we put in our own way. What is cluttering our path? What are some ways we can clear that clutter to make our way easier to navigate?

Chapter Seven
Rest Stop Stories—Part Two

It's probably as good a time as any to stretch our legs and get some more fresh air. One of the cool things about calling baseball games in the major leagues is the chance to meet so many "big" names. I've already told you about Rush Limbaugh. He was just one of what turned out to be a steady parade of celebrities that would stop by for a chat in my nine years of doing major league baseball.

The "Other" Armstrong

Sure, there are those rare times we have a guest for a basketball or football game. I once had the chance to visit with Lance Armstrong during a Texas Longhorns game in Austin. He noticed my name and wondered if we were related. We're not. Besides, my Schwinn couldn't keep up with him for more than about twenty yards.

Last year Reid and I were visiting with Texas Coach Rick Barnes about his association with Lance. Coach Barnes told us he sees him all the time in Austin. In fact, just that morning he said passed Lance on the bike trail. Reid and I were stunned!

"You passed him?" We asked in unison. "Well, sure," he responded, "he was going the opposite way on the path."

So basketball and football have their moments, but baseball is the best for getting into long conversations with someone. The pace of the game lends itself to an extended visit.

Through the years, I had the chance to visit with Mr. October, Reggie Jackson. Lou Brock, the speedster from St. Louis stopped by. Hank Aaron in Atlanta. I met the Willies, Mays and McCovey in San Francisco. Dave Winfield in San Diego. My boyhood heroes, Al Kaline and Ernie Harwell in Detroit. Bob Feller in Cleveland. Virtually every city we went to would produce one Hall-of-Famer or another.

Kid Rock and Pamela Anderson

I have always liked it best when we had the chance to visit with celebrities outside of the game of baseball. One such occasion happened in 2001 in Los Angeles. I was with the Colorado Rockies then. We were at Chavez Ravine to play the Dodgers. With its proximity to Hollywood, it's not unusual to spot a movie star or someone from the music industry.

On this particular night in late August, Kid Rock and Pamela Anderson were spotted, sitting together behind home plate. I was obviously familiar with who they were. Their romance was all the rage at the time. You couldn't go by a newsstand without seeing them on somebody's cover. I may have seen an episode or two of *"Baywatch,"* but I couldn't name one Kid Rock song. I know he's talented, but I must admit, I didn't have any of his music on my ipod.

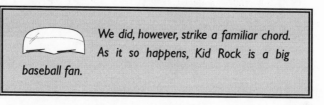

We did, however, strike a familiar chord. As it so happens, Kid Rock is a big baseball fan.

Somehow, our producer convinced them to join us in the booth. I was never more unprepared to interview someone. I started my chat with Kid Rock, "So, Mr. Rock..." That's when the producer got in my ear with, "Jeez Dave, you don't have to call him Mister Rock. How square are you anyway?" Pretty square as it would turn out. We did, however, strike a familiar chord. As it so happens, Kid Rock is a big baseball fan. Who knew? And he was a fan of the Detroit Tigers! Talk about a common ground.

So I began to ask him all about his memories of Al Kaline and Norm Cash and Denny McLain and the 1968 World Champion Tigers. The year they came back from a 3-1 deficit to beat Bob Gibson and the St. Louis Cardinals. Mickey Lolich became a legend in the Motor City, winning three games in the Fall Classic. I couldn't wait to talk to Mr. Rock about all the details and intricacies of this series.

How they moved Mickey Stanley from center field to shortstop to get a more potent offensive attack on the field. I was armed and ready to take this conversation to another level. But he cut me off by responding, "Well, my dad loved that team. I was thinking more of Alan Trammel and Kirk Gibson from 1984." Boy, did I feel old! And square.

You're probably wondering about Pamela Anderson. She didn't say much. And that was just fine with the large male population now congregating in our booth. I think every writer from the press box was now crowded in there. Her attire looked like something she would wear on the set of "Baywatch." This didn't help keep the population down. I had already used up my yearly allotment of embarrassment with Mr. Rock, so I wasn't about to ask her any questions.

You should also know I was celebrating my 25th wedding anniversary on this very night. My wife was in attendance. What a good sport. She took pictures of everything. I don't think either of us ever planned to join the paparazzi corps for our anniversary. But it will go down in history as the most memorable one.

From Plains to Some Plain Talk

Earlier that same year, we were in Atlanta to play the Braves. I always liked to go to Turner Field. A beautiful new stadium. Home to the franchise that won 14 straight division titles. An amazing run. Talk about consistent excellence. The Braves would be a great study for someone wanting to write a thesis on sustaining a winning attitude throughout an organization.

> *Talk about consistent excellence. The Braves would be a great study for someone wanting to write a thesis on sustaining a winning attitude throughout an organization.*

From our perch behind home plate, I noticed former President Jimmy Carter sitting in the stands. Our producer cut through the red tape and Secret Service. In a matter of minutes, President Carter was with us in the booth. Protocol says that when the President is in your presence, you stand. It's not just polite-it's expected. So my partner, George Frazier, and I stood. George is about 6'3". I stand 6'6". President Carter is maybe 5'7". It made it appear we were "towering" over the President. He didn't seem to mind, but I remember being very uncomfortable.

President Carter couldn't have been more cordial. We spent the better part of an inning listening to him tell about his love for the game of baseball. And, in particular, his love for the Atlanta Braves.

> We got into a great discussion about President Carter's humanitarian efforts. Efforts that would be honored with a Nobel Peace Prize in 2002.

I was more comfortable talking politics than music with Kid Rock. So we got into a great discussion about President Carter's humanitarian efforts. Efforts that would be honored with a Nobel Peace Prize in 2002. We also talked about his work with Habitat for Humanity. It was like visiting with a long, lost relative. It was great; I just wish he had invited us to sit.

Well time for us to sit back in the car, and get back on the road.

Chapter Eight
Changing Lanes and Careers

That was a great place to stop for lunch. Quick in and out, but not fast food. I've lost a little weight recently; about fifty pounds, and I'd like to keep it off. Now, if I do stop for fast food, I'm just as likely to get a salad and not a burger or fries. Plus, the place where we just ate had great restrooms. Clean, with automatic paper towel dispensers. And a door that pushed out, perfect.

Football Luncheon at Arrowhead Stadium

Quick story about fast food before we change lanes. I emceed a luncheon a few years ago at the Truman Sports Complex. It was a Football Kick-off Luncheon at Arrowhead Stadium, the home of the Kansas City Chiefs. But this was a college football luncheon, not for the pros in the National Football League.

On the dais was Mark Mangino, the head coach of the Kansas Jayhawks. Bill Snyder, the head coach of the Kansas State Wildcats. Plus two coaches from NCAA Division II. Chuck Broyles from Pittsburg

State and Mel Tjeerdsma (pronounced Church-ma) from Northwest Missouri State.

Before lunch, Coach Broyles was telling me about his trip to Kansas City from Pittsburg, a small town in the southeast corner of Kansas. He mentioned that he always brought two shirts along because he invariably spilled some sort of fast food or drink on one of them. I asked if I could tell this story to the gathering of about 250 avid college football fans. He agreed so I did. Coach Tjeerdsma got up after my remarks and told how he had to turn around a few miles outside of Warrensburg, the home of the Bearcats. He had to go back to his house to get a new shirt. He had spilled coffee all over the one he was wearing. When he was done, I got back up and said, "Hey Guys, when you get to Division One, your courtesy cars come with cup holders." They were kind enough to take the gentle ribbing in stride. By the way, both gentlemen are terrific coaches running programs that are perennially vying for a national championship.

Now that lunch is over, it's time to change lanes and talk about things that detour our careers. Life is a lot different today. Gone are the days when someone stays with one company for an entire career. Then, after thirty or so years of loyal service, collects his or her pension along with a gold watch.

Changing Lanes and Careers

Career changes are now the norm. Loyalty is a two way street. Employers are often looking for an exit sign when it comes to their employees. Employees are constantly checking the career map to see if there is a better route. Detours pop up on the horizon all the time. Especially if you pick a volatile career like broadcasting. But it really doesn't matter what field you're in anymore. Lane changes go with the territory of doing business today. **I have friends in all kinds of different endeavors of life. I can't think of one that hasn't faced some sort of career change.**

> *Men and women all over this country are toting their little cardboard boxes with all their portable valuables out to the parking lot all the time.*

Sometimes it's self-induced. Looking for a better situation. More money, bigger upside, better working environment, closer to home. Whatever.

Sometimes we have no choice in the matter. We're let go because management needs to downsize. Or they want to go in "another direction." It happens. Men and women all over this country are toting their little cardboard boxes with all their portable valuables out to the parking lot all the time. It happens everyday, and it's across the board. Job change takes no prisoners. It's an equal opportunity lane change.

In the quarter of a century I've been in this business of broadcasting, we've lived in seven different cities. Most of the lane changes were voluntary. Career advancement. I've been very fortunate. I still find it to be a remarkable journey to go from KGGF in Coffeyville to Major League Baseball, the NFL, the Big 12 Network and ESPN.

Sometimes the lane changes have involved a little nudge. And a couple of times I was forced to take a detour.

From Coffeyville to Chanute...Exactly When Do We Hit the Big Time?

I thought we'd pick up my career after the Coffeyville disaster. A week after my little "incident," I found myself, and all of my portable valuables, on 169 Highway heading for Chanute. They didn't call it a firing at KGGF, but they were kind enough to "re-locate" me to KKOY about 45 miles to the north. It was a nudge to the other lane.

On the short drive there, I had a little pep talk with myself. "Look, Dave, you're getting a fresh start. No one in Chanute knows about your little mishaps. This is your chance to get your career on the right track." I was really getting myself fired up for this new challenge. I was about ready to invoke the spirit of Knute Rockne and the "Gipper" when I pulled into the parking lot at KKOY. Basically it came down to this: either make it here, or go back to hauling windshields at the Glass Factory. This was the end of the road.

Something happened as soon as I stepped into the station to start my new job. First of all, I met the owner, Dale McCoy. I would soon find out that he would be much more than a boss. Dale would become a trusted friend and mentor. He shook my hand with great enthusiasm. Mr. McCoy could make Dale Carnegie negative. He was a small man with a big spirit. About 5'7" tall and about 150 pounds. He had a twinkle in his eye and a spring in his step. I liked him immediately.

All the fear and trepidation I experienced in Coffeyville had melted away in an instant. I felt welcomed. It's even fair to say I felt loved. It was like I was given the secret handshake at the first meeting. Welcomed to the family with open arms. A few minutes later I was ushered into the studio, and I was on the air.

> *This was my moment of truth. A dream that started to form at that kitchen table listening to Ernie Harwell on the radio describing Tiger baseball was on the line.*

This was my moment of truth. A dream that started to form at that kitchen table listening to Ernie Harwell on the radio describing Tiger baseball was on the line. Four years of college and one failed attempt in my rear view mirror. But looking now through the windshield, this whole experience felt different. I was my old confident self again. My voice was stronger and bolder with the first words that came out of my mouth and through my lips. I had made an amazing transformation literally overnight. It was a quantum leap in my career.

When my shift was over, Dale came busting through the doors of the studio and gave me a big bear hug. It felt great, and I knew right then that I was in the right business and in the right place. I knew everything was going to be okay. By the way, the station manager from KGGF heard my show on the radio that day. He called later to say congratulations while wondering why I didn't sound like that in Coffeyville.

Confidence is the Key

How was I able to make such a startling turn around that quickly? In a word, confidence. I didn't have any at all at KGGF. Dale McCoy gave me just the dose I needed when I first entered his station. I'm a big believer in confidence as a huge factor in the success or failure of an individual. It certainly has played a big role in my own career. And I've seen it have the same effect on countless others through the years.

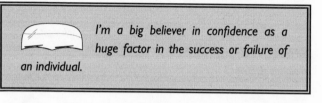

I'm a big believer in confidence as a huge factor in the success or failure of an individual.

I don't understand the boss or superior who wants to undermine the confidence of those working for them. It seems counterproductive to me. I'm not Dr. Phil, but I think it stems from a lack of confidence by that boss. They're so worried about their workers outperforming them that they always try to keep a thumb on top of the employees' heads to squelch their growth. It just doesn't make any sense.

From Swap 'N Save to Running the Show

That certainly wasn't the case at KKOY with Dale McCoy. Time passed quickly in Chanute. I was having fun. I was valued, and it felt great. My radio show was from nine in the morning until noon. Part of my shift included a show called "Swap and Save." It was basically the classified section of the newspaper on the air. People would call in and advertise the stuff they had to sell. It was pretty hokey. But I really enjoyed talking to the people of Chanute everyday.

"Swap and Save" became so popular that we expanded it from a half-hour to a full hour. We probably could have gone even longer. All our phone lines were tied up the entire time. It became more than want ads. It was like the town water cooler where we could discuss almost anything, and often did.

One time my brother was in town for a visit. He was on spring break from his college in Texas. He called in to "Swap and Save," disguising his voice. I had no idea it was him. He drawled on the phone, "Ah, yeah, I got me two rabbits to sell." It sounded pretty much like any other local farmer in the area so I wasn't suspicious. He went on, "Wait a minute, make that four rabbits." Before I could ask for a phone number where people could reach him, he continued. "Now wait a dadgum second. Make that eight rabbits! Hey! Make them stop doing that!" We both laughed like crazy. It wasn't until I got home later in the day that he revealed himself as the caller. Another reason I loved him. What a prankster.

 It was a big undertaking, an enormous challenge, and I loved every minute of it.
I love a challenge.

In a short time at KKOY, I was promoted to the position of Program Director. We took on the task of changing the entire format of our FM station. We also fine-tuned the sound of the AM side.It was a big undertaking, an enormous challenge, and I loved every minute of it. I love a challenge. And I learned so much.

One of the things I learned about leadership from Dale during this time has wound up benefiting me to this day. What I learned was, if you want your employees to really "buy into" a plan, make them believe the idea is theirs in the first place. In other words, have the confidence to give them the credit. They work harder, better and smarter.

Plus I found that they came up with all sorts of their own great thoughts on how to improve both stations. Confidence was bursting at the seams. It was a great place to work. An extremely productive environment.

It all started with Dale McCoy. He was a master motivator and innovator. Sadly, he passed away a few years ago after dealing with heart problems for a long period of time. He literally saved my career, and I owe him a huge debt of gratitude.

Looking to the Horizon For New Challenges

I'm always looking for a new challenge. I've discovered that if I stay in the same lane too long, I get bogged down in traffic. There's no room for advancement. I get stuck in a rut. I don't see the scenery around me; I just see the enormous

18-wheeler over my hood. I even smell its diesel fumes.

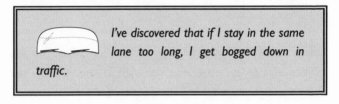

I've discovered that if I stay in the same lane too long, I get bogged down in traffic.

It's not that I've jumped all around like a real life game of "Frogger." After all, I stayed three years in Chanute. That's about two more than what's normal for a young broadcaster at a small market station. I really didn't want to leave. I loved it there so much.

From Chanute to Hays—Still No Big Time

But I had always wanted to try my hand at television. It was Dale who encouraged me to pursue that goal. He was kind enough to say he didn't want to lose me, but he also wanted what was best for my career. He treated me more like one of his sons than an employee. He helped me find a job at KAYS-TV in Hays, Kansas.

I know most of you are getting out your atlas to see where all these little towns are in the Sunflower State. I'll save you the trouble. Hays is in the northwestern part of Kansas. Right on I-70, about two hours from the border of Colorado. It's flat, windy, and very Bohemian. Settlers from Germany populated the area centuries ago for its rich farmland. These were great folks who worked hard and played hard, too. If you ever get the chance, attend Oktoberfest some fall in Hays, America. You won't be disappointed.

The station itself was really good, but it was hard for me to replace the feeling I had in Chanute. I missed my old friends. Still, I knew this was best for my career. The lane change was something I had to do. I was starting to get stagnant in Chanute. I was beginning to choke on the diesel fumes. I needed to get out from behind that semi and get a fresh view. I found it on I-70 at exit 159.

I got up to speed pretty quickly on the television side. I started off doing the weather, then shifted to sports within a month or so. But this was another small market station, and you had to do a little bit of everything. That included tours of the station for local Boy Scout troops, or hosting the noon show. The hours were brutal. Twelve hours a day, six days a week. Plus, the pay was still pitiful. Barely above the poverty line. I was watching some of my buddies from college in other fields making much more, and I started to resent it a little bit. I still loved what I was doing but felt the need to be on a bigger stage.

So one night after the late newscast was over, I went to my desk and wrote out a letter of resignation. There was no turning back; I was going to make my move after being in Hays for only eleven months, three days and seventeen hours. As soon as I finished the letter, I bravely walked down the hall to the station manager's office. After giving the letter a final stare, I knelt down and slid it under his locked door. He could read all about it the next morning. I was outta there.

I went home to tell my wife what I had done. She was supportive but also nervous about the consequences of being without any job. After a long discussion into the wee hours of the morning, she convinced me that the right thing to do was to get another job first before quitting the one I already had. That sounded like good sound advice. Okay, that's settled. I'll start looking for a new position the first thing in the morning.

Wait! Oh no! The letter! So at four in the morning, I sneak back over to KAYS-TV. Here I am, a grown man, on his hands and knees in front of the station manager's office again. With bent wire coat hanger in hand, I was finally able to "fish" the letter out from under locked door.

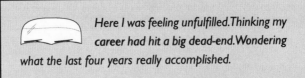

Here I was feeling unfulfilled. Thinking my career had hit a big dead-end. Wondering what the last four years really accomplished.

The next day, I'm sitting at my desk in the middle of the afternoon. Depressed. I was tired of giving tours of the station for Johnny's birthday party. I guess I was tired of not mattering, or thinking I didn't. Here I was feeling unfulfilled. Thinking my career had hit a big dead-end. Wondering what the last four years really accomplished.

Not really caring to see the big picture. The picture that I was still in a career I loved, just not in the place I wanted to be at that time. And on top of it all, it made no practical sense to just walk out the door. Even though I really wanted to.

As an aside, this feeling had nothing to do with the folks in Hays. It had nothing to do with the people at the television station. They were all terrific. If KAYS had been my first job out of college, it would have been the greatest experience ever. It's just that after four years I had the real urge to test the waters in a bigger pond.

For the moment though, I sat at my desk and sulked. Just then, and I'm not making this up, the phone rang. It was Bill Sykes, the program director at a TV station in Wichita. He was offering me a job! Talk about a modern day miracle! It was time to change lanes again, and I couldn't wait to put my blinker on to signal the move.

From Hays to Wichita—We're Getting Closer

In Wichita, I worked at KARD-TV. Soon after I joined them, they changed the call letters to

KSNW-TV. Working there was one of the best things that has ever happened to me in my career. Most of what I am today as a broadcaster is due in large part to the great experience I gained there.

> Most of what I am today as a broadcaster is due in large part to the great experience I gained there.

First of all, I worked for a great man in Webb Smith. He was very much like Dale. Very warm, very generous. He was the Sports Director and did the sportscasts Monday through Friday. I handled the weekends. I would also file stories that he would run on his shows during the week. More often than not, I would get a phone call from Webb after a piece had run. He wanted to thank me for the effort. I don't know if I ever really told him how much that meant to me. He continued the confidence building project that was started in Chanute. He is about twenty years my senior and is more like a big brother. A really, really great big brother.

Within a few weeks of arriving in Wichita, the Ringling Brothers Barnum and Bailey Circus was coming to town. Trains were bringing the animals. There was going to be a parade from the train station to the Kansas Coliseum. They needed local celebrities to ride the elephants in the parade. Since I was the new guy, I was chosen. I think this is what they call rookie hazing.

The Barnum and Bailey Circus

Elephants don't smell like roses on a good day. Imagine their stench after riding in an un-air conditioned train in the middle of summer in Kansas. Nevertheless, I was hoisted up on this big, smelly beast. I tried to smile at all the folks lining the streets on the parade route. But it wasn't easy to do that while holding my nose at the same time. It took what seemed like an eternity to reach our final destination. All the elephants gathered in the same spot. All twenty or so of them. And they all relieved themselves at the same time. They must not have gone for days. I looked down from my perch on top of one of these creatures. I was staring at the Urine River. Their handler, wearing big knee-high rubber boots, was screaming at me to get off of his elephant. You could see my dilemma. For a guy who doesn't even want to go near a public restroom, this was a worst-case scenario. I've psychologicallyblockedoutwhathappenednextor, I promise, I'd tell you.

In the Right Lane at the Right Time

After this little initiation, I was part of the team. After a couple of years our station decided to get heavily involved in local sports production. And their decision has really helped shape the rest of my career.

You can call it fate, or happenstance, or just pure luck. But I was definitely in the right place at the right time. This was a classic case of outside influences determining my path. I had no factor in their decision, and yet I benefited the most. They changed my life's journey; I just went along for the ride.

This was before the time that ESPN cornered the market of sports production. Local stations still made up a large chunk of sports programming. Our station bought a recreational vehicle, yes, an R-V. Our engineers gutted it and made a production van. We were on the road. Webb wanted to stay in the studio so I got the opportunity to do the play-by-play for hundreds of events for the next few years. It was a chance to get real, practical experience. It was invaluable. It was on-the-job training at its best.

I really didn't know what I was doing. Sort of learning on the fly. I studied others doing play-by-play. Men like Bob Costas and Dick Enberg. I didn't copy them, but it's safe to say I tried to emulate them.

Rubbing Elbows with Dick Enberg...Wow!

I got the chance to meet Mr. Enberg when he came to Lawrence to broadcast a Kansas Jayhawks basketball game for NBC. He was one third of perhaps the best team to ever broadcast college basketball. Dick worked with Billy Packer and the late

Al McGuire. They were terrific together. Very entertaining and informative.

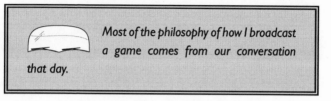

Most of the philosophy of how I broadcast a game comes from our conversation that day.

I used to do a feature on our local sportscasts called "Armstrong's Album." I used this platform as an excuse to interview Mr. Enberg. He was generous to spend some time with me and answer a lot of my questions. Most of the philosophy of how I broadcast a game came from our conversation that day.

Dick Enberg is known for his signature call, "Oh My!" I asked him why he said that particular phrase at an exciting moment in a game. He said it was so he could put an "exclamation point" on the end of the play and then let the crowd take over. That made a lot of sense.

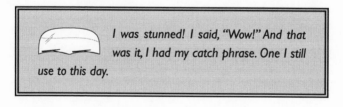

I was stunned! I said, "Wow!" And that was it, I had my catch phrase. One I still use to this day.

So I went in search of my catch phrase. I tried, "Oh, Gee, that was swell!" Yeah I know, pretty weak. A friend of mine in Texas says, "Oh, Mamma! Hold on to your pants!" So, that was taken.

Then one night in 1984, I was calling a game at historic Allen Fieldhouse at Kansas. The great Danny Manning, who would four years later go on to lead KU to their fourth national championship, was just a freshman. Cedric Hunter was the point guard, and he lobbed a pass in the general direction of the basket. Danny came flying out of the rafters from near the "Beware of the Phog" sign to grab it and slam it through the hoop. I was stunned! I said, "Wow!" And that was it, I had my catch phrase. One I still use to this day.

Lane changes. Detours. Life. All of it goes together to create a landscape that is sometimes beautiful. Sometimes stormy. At the end of the day, it's the journey that's important, not the destination.

Time to Reflect—
Pit Stop #5

This is going to be our biggest pit stop of the day. We need not gas only, but also four new tires. Good thing we've got a great pit crew to get us back in the race as soon as possible.

Point of Interest—
Confidence is the Key

Have you ever done any "people watching"? It's one of my favorite pastimes. One trait that you can spot a thousand miles away on someone is confidence. It's apparent in the way they carry themselves. In the way they walk or talk. It's very appealing to us all.

What's keeping you from being your most confident today? Are you worried about the opinions of others? Are you lacking a certain skill? While we can't sway public opinion, we can improve our own ability to complete a task. As we get more comfortable, confidence is a natural by-product of our efforts.

Point of Interest—
Always Look for a New Challenge

The only way we can truly grow is to be on a constant lookout for a new challenge. Sometimes we get so comfortable in our environment that we become complacent. Stale. It might be safe to stay right where we are, but there's no new scenery.

One of my favorite expressions is "You can't get the fruit unless you go out on the limb." Even though it's sometimes scary, let's make a plan today to look for new opportunities.

Point of Interest—
Sometimes You Just Happen To Be in the Right Lane

Some days are just easy. Why are we surprised when this happens? I'm not a great golfer. So when I start a round with a couple of birdies, I'm almost afraid to shoot a low score. I can't get out of my own way. This is the wrong attitude. When things are going our way, let's promise not to look for sharks in the water but just ride the wave.

Chapter Nine
Driver's Training-Mentoring

What a great journey we're on. I hope you're enjoying it as much as I am. You are wonderful company.

My kids are pretty grown up now. One is already in college, and the other one in high school. They're both terrific. But they couldn't be more different if they came from two different parts of the planet. Their personality differences carry over into the way they drive. I should know, I taught both of them the rules of the road.

Driver's Training

I learned to drive, like most people, in a driver's ed course. Only with ours, we had a driving range where the top speed was fifteen miles per hour. You hardly even had to use the gas pedal to go that fast. I remember getting two "speeding" tickets for going about 17. Really reckless stuff.

I didn't get out on a real road until after I got my license. My dad went with me to the DMV to get it. You know, the same dad that was used to going at high speeds in a Big Red Fire Truck. After I got my picture taken and got my permit, we hit the highway. I got on the service ramp on Southfield Freeway near Joy Road. I was going 30 miles an hour! I had never in my life driven this fast. I could feel the wind blowing through my hair. I felt free. And scared.

Then my dad instructed me to get on the freeway. I idled down the ramp, still going 30. That was fast enough as far as I was concerned. For some reason, other cars on the road were honking their horns and making rather nasty gestures in my direction. At this point my dad is urging, no he's pleading, with me to go faster. Somehow I couldn't put my foot any further down on the gas pedal. At his insistence, we got off at the next exit, still going 30. I fully expected him to get out of the car at any second, cross the median, and hitch a ride home.

I wasn't going to put my kids through this same drivers education experience. I wanted them to learn how to drive out in the real world, not some range. So we enrolled them in "Daddy Driver's Ed." What was I thinking? Talk about a white-knuckle experience. I'd sit in the passenger seat resisting the urge to constantly grab the wheel. I had my thumb cocked, ready to hitch a ride anywhere when things got a little hairy. Like father, like son.

Actually, both of my kids took to driving pretty quickly. Although it was a little while before we ventured out onto the freeway. Once my daughter figured out which one was the gas pedal, she was off and flying. My son is more conservative. He likes to stay in his own lane and drive the speed limit. I'm proud to say, they're both good, defensive drivers.

Mentoring is Cool!

In a sense, once we've reached a certain stage in our careers, we become parents to the next generation. I think it's important to "pay it forward." To pass on the knowledge we've gleaned through life's experiences. We get the opportunity to teach others to drive.

Gordie Howe and the Great One

> *I felt this gave me a slight edge over other sportscasters in the city. Most of them had never seen a hockey game before. They didn't know icing the puck from icing a cake.*

When I was in Wichita, the city welcomed a new hockey team to town. The Wichita Wind. It was a minor league club affiliated with the Edmonton Oilers.

Since I grew up in Detroit, "Hockey Town," I felt this gave me a slight edge over other sportscasters in the city. Most of them had never seen a hockey game before. They didn't know icing the puck from icing a cake.

The Oilers decided to bring one of their budding superstars to Wichita to promote the team. His name? Wayne Gretzky. The Great One. Only at this stage of his career, he was just getting started. He was only 19. Everyone knew he was special, but no one could have predicted how great he would become.

The Oilers also decided to bring in another super-star. Gordie Howe. Yep, the same Gordie Howe who scored more goals than anyone in the history of the game. (Until Gretzky broke his records.) The same man who played more than a quarter of a century in the National Hockey League. The same man who skated for the Detroit Red Wings at The Olympiad. Number nine. Another boyhood hero of mine. I knew his background. I followed his career. "Followed" isn't a strong enough word. I studied it. I documented it. In fact, I wrote an English paper about Gordie Howe.

So all of us are waiting our turn to interview these two men. I'm not shy, but I was extremely nervous about talking to Mr. Howe. There he was, in living person. I wasn't just seeing him on television or from the balcony of the Olympiad. He was stand-ing right next to me. I felt like I was ten again, ask-ing for his autograph. Sweaty palms. Nervous tone to my voice. Stammering words.

Gordie could sense my tension and immediately put me at ease. I stumbled something about being from Detroit, and he seized on this to help comfort me.

You're probably wondering what this has to do with mentoring. I'm getting to that. I glanced over and noticed Wayne Gretzky was equally nervous in talking to Mr. Howe. Gordie helped put Wayne at ease as well.

> *Gordie put his arm around "Gretz" and told him how great he could be. He shared insights. He told Wayne that someday he would eclipse all of his own records.*

Here's Wayne Gretzky, age 19, and yours truly stammering our way through this conversation. Gordie put his arm around "Gretz" and told him how great he could be. He shared insights. He told Wayne that someday he would eclipse all of his own records. Of course he did. But I've always wondered if the genesis of that dream wasn't born that day in Wichita.

Mr. Howe then invited both of us to lunch. I felt like the luckiest guy in the world. For the better part of the next two hours, I sat between Gordie Howe and Wayne Gretzky. The two greatest hockey players in the history of the game.

Wayne and I sat there, totally enthralled. It's safe to say, Gordie mentored us both that day.

By now, I felt more comfortable. I started to remember all the facts from my childhood as they pertained to Mr. Howe. I was able to get him to tell some amazing stories about his life and career. Wayne and I sat there, totally enthralled. It's safe to say, Gordie mentored us both that day. My only regret is I don't have any photos from that experience. But I sure have stockpiled plenty of mental pictures of one of the best days of my life.

Sometimes I have to pinch myself. Shagging flies with George Brett at Tiger Stadium, having lunch with Gordie and the Great One. Dream stuff. I'm a lucky, lucky man!

On the Air with a Rookie Partner

Now that I've been in this business of broadcasting for over a quarter of a century, I've found great pleasure in sharing my experiences with others. In my work for the folks at ESPNU, I'm sort of known as the play-by-play guy that works best with the "rookies." I'm honored that they feel that way.

> *In my work for the folks at ESPNU, I'm sort of known as the play-by-play guy that works best with the "rookies." I'm honored that they feel that way.*

A lot of times, I'll get the new guy assigned as my partner. The player or coach who has just finished his or her career and wants to take a stab at being an analyst. They have all the knowledge from the game; they just might not know the best way to share that with a viewing audience. It's not my job to train them, but I enjoy the challenge. It's like an unspoken mandate from my superiors to give the new guy a helping hand. Some others in my position only want to work with seasoned professionals. Hey, don't get me wrong, I like that too. But I also enjoy taking someone who is pretty rough around the edges. It's fun to help carve them into becoming a good analyst.

Most of these men or women are just thrown into the deep end without a clue as to how to swim. There's no real training ground. I guess the executive producers feel there are plenty of folks who want to do this; if one analyst doesn't work out, they'll just go to plan "B." Just this year, I worked with a new basketball analyst for a two-day tournament down in College Station, Texas. The Aggies of Texas A & M were hosting. My rookie partner was well prepared. I could sense he really wanted to do a great job. That's half the battle. If they want to put in the work, I'm more than willing to help them.

When we went on the air though, I could also tell he was uncomfortable. To be honest, his first night was rough. He was pretty bland. After the show, he wanted to know how he did. I could have gone one of two ways here. I could have easily said, "Oh, you did fine. We'll see you tomorrow." But I could tell how much he wanted to succeed in this arena. So I told him the truth. "Honestly, you weren't very good," I said. I know that sounds harsh. But I've found through the years that athletes and coaches are used to frank talk. They want the truth. Not the sugarcoated, watered-down version. I went on, "Look, tomorrow night you've got to bring more energy. When you played, you were expected to score. On a television broadcast, it's important for the analyst to score points."

My role as a play-by-play man, at its best, is when I'm able to set up my partner. Throw him a lob pass that he can slam into the hoop. In my view, if the analyst is getting all the assists, the broadcast is backwards.

The next night, he came out and was a different guy. He had more energy. He had his confidence, his swagger. The points he made were more poignant. He scored. Afterwards, he sent me a thank-you note. A written thank-you note. I've had it framed. One of my proudest moments and one of the great joys I've been able to experience through the years.

Working with the Master of Manhattan—Wildcat Coach Jack Hartman

Several years ago, I had the chance to work with the late Jack Hartman after he finished his time as coach of the Kansas State basketball team. K-State enjoyed some of the best years in their history when Coach Hartman was in charge.

The first time I ever met him was when I went up to Manhattan from Wichita to cover the Wildcats for KSNW-TV. I wasn't there to broadcast the game. I was just doing a story on the team, getting interviews and such. They had a great team back then, led by All-America forward Rolando Blackmon.

During practice, Coach Hartman was in a foul mood and barked in our direction to get our camera and ourselves out of Ahearn Fieldhouse. We did. Quickly.

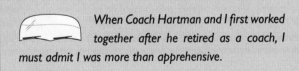 *When Coach Hartman and I first worked together after he retired as a coach, I must admit I was more than apprehensive.*

When we first worked together after he retired as a coach, I must admit I was more than apprehensive. I remembered that day at practice. But he couldn't have been nicer. He was like the best grandpa you could imagine.

He was having a difficult time making the transition from coaching to the broadcast booth. After working with him a few times, I really got a sense of his growing frustration. He told me he wasn't sure he was cut out for this line of work. I didn't want him to give up; I really liked working with him.

We were at Oklahoma State in Stillwater, his alma mater. He played for the legendary coach, Henry Iba. Mr. Iba, if you will. Before the game began, I turned to Coach Hartman and said, "Coach, I don't want you to broadcast this game." "What? You want me to quit just before the opening tip-off?" He responded. "No," I said. "I want you to coach this game over the air. I want you to think like a coach. I want you to talk like a coach. Without the bad language." He did exactly that and it was magic. Brilliant stuff, really.

> "I want you to coach this game over the air. I want you to think like a coach. I want you to talk like a coach. Without the bad language." He did exactly that and it was magic. Brilliant stuff, really.

The game was close, and he took us into both huddles and told us exactly what he would be saying if that were his team. He made the transition from coach to broadcaster that day. I'm telling you, I learned more about the game of basketball in that one afternoon than I have in all the days since. Maybe the best part was, he had fun. He lit up like a little kid around the holidays. He even gave me a hug afterwards and said thanks. Another proud and yet humble moment.

Coach Hartman to the Rescue

I'm glad I made a friend in Coach Hartman. He would come to my aid later that same year. At the end of every basketball season, the conference holds a tournament. This was still in the days of the Big Eight Conference. They hadn't yet welcomed in the four schools from Texas to form the Big Twelve. Each year, the tournament was held at Kemper Arena in Kansas City.

It was 1989, my first year calling the event. I worked the previous year, but didn't get to announce the games in March. I was very excited to get this assignment. I felt my career definitely heading in the right direction.

On the day before the actual Big Eight Tournament began playing games, each team would work out at Kemper Arena. This was a great chance for the reporters to talk with the players and coaches as they filed their stories to preview the action.

It was also a great chance for those of us broadcasting to get another story or two we could relate to our viewing audience.

> *I was still a bit intimidated by their long-time coach Norm Stewart. He is a big man, and back then, he could turn on the charm, or let you have it.*

Things were going smoothly until the Missouri Tigers took the court. I had already broadcast a few of the Tigers games that year. I was still a bit intimidated by their long-time coach Norm Stewart. He is a big man, and back then, he could turn on the charm, or let you have it. On this day, he chose the latter.

Without provocation, Coach Stewart "stormed" over to our location court-side. He thrust his finger into my chest while shouting, "What you said earlier this year about Anthony Peeler is a load of you-know-what!"

I was rubbing my chest while searching my memory banks for what I possibly could have said about his talented guard that would have the Coach so upset. I finally just said, "Coach, I don't know what you're talking about. I've never said anything bad about Anthony Peeler. I think he's a terrific player."

Coach Stewart, still poking, said, "I heard what you said on the videotape. You said 'Peeler leans in and draws the contact. He'll go to the line to make it a three-point play.' That's what you said." "Yeah, I did say that. What's so bad about that Coach?" I asked.

"Well, now every referee in the league is looking for that move, and he's not getting the calls anymore. It's all your fault!" Coach Stewart fumed.

I didn't know what to say. Just then, Coach Hartman stepped in front of me. He looked up at Norm and said, "Hey, leave this guy alone! He's the best!"

Norm Stewart walked away chuckling. I don't know if the whole thing was an act. All I know is thanks to Coach Hartman, Norm and I have been close ever since. He's treated me like a friend. A classic case of mentoring paying off for the mentor.

Shut Up and Listen

I've found that one of the keys to teaching newcomers the craft of broadcasting is listening to them. I pay strict attention to what the analyst is saying. Too often, we get caught up with what we want to say next. We don't take the time to hear what the other person is saying. Or trying to say. They might know how to play or coach the game; but sometimes they have trouble articulating that. I try to ask them questions to help coax the information from them in a more comfortable manner.

I've found that when I truly listen to what my partner has to say about an athletic event, I really learn much more about the game. My partner is more comfortable, and the listener is the big beneficiary.

Since they've played or coached, they're used to the interview process. So in the beginning I turn the game into a long question and answer session. As they gain confidence, they can then make the transition from the passenger side of the car to a seat behind the wheel. When driver's training is over, so to speak, that's when they become invaluable. That's when they become broadcasters.

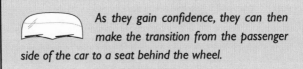

As they gain confidence, they can then make the transition from the passenger side of the car to a seat behind the wheel.

It's no different in business. New hires need to be trained. They need to be shown the ropes. But at some point, they also need to be able to drive on their own. To go on a solo journey without an instructor. If they constantly need supervision, they're of no real value to an organization.

At some point down the road, we have the opportunity to give something back. It takes confidence to be a mentor. It takes patience. It takes the ability to stop and listen. I know it's easier to do our own thing. But we can be generous. Take it from me. The rewards you get when helping someone else are priceless.

Time to Reflect—
Pit Stop #6

We're coming around the last turn, just this one last pit stop to get a little gas in the tank before we take the checkered flag.

Point of Interest—
Mentoring is a Gift...To Both Parties!

My sister's husband is an excellent fisherman. Or at least everyone says he is. I've never actually seen him catch anything. At family gatherings, he'll sneak off with rod and reel in hand to some fishing hole. He usually comes back, hours later, with stories of the "one that got away." (I've always suspected that he's taking a nap somewhere.)

All kidding aside, he must know something, because his son really is a great fisherman. One of my brother-in-law's great joys is passing on his passion for fishing to the next generation. He shows great patience, even when he gets a hook in the back of the neck from an errant cast of his fishing partner.

The smile on someone's face when the light goes on and they "get it" is priceless. I've talked to many retired athletes. Men and women who have enjoyed great success in different arenas around the world. They all get greater joy out of watching their own children than anything they accomplished on the playing field.

When we help someone along the road, we create a friend for life. That's a win-win. Who can you mentor today?

Point of Interest—
Listening is Better Than Talking

I know that sounds weird coming from a broadcaster. After all, we're known for having a rather large vocal capacity.

I'm paid to talk, but I've found it's just as important for me to listen. I need to hear the producer in my ear, whispering cues on what direction we're heading. I need to listen to my on-air partner so I can help him or her reach their full potential. Sometimes I need to listen to them both at the same time! No wonder it seems like we talk out of both sides of our mouth.

We can all do a better job of listening. It's one of the keys to mentoring. It's one of the keys of better leadership. Are we listening? Or are we only concerned about ourselves?

Chapter Ten
Coming Home

I really don't want this trip to end, but we've almost made it back home. It's been a lot of fun to travel together. I know we'll do it again soon.

> *When you spread out the map of life the way we have, it's really cool to look back and see how we got from here to there.*

When you spread out the map of life the way we have, it's really cool to look back and see how we got from here to there. We've shared a lot. We've talked about looking through the windshield and not the rear-view mirror. How important it is to keep our focus on what's in front of us and not what's in the past. We've chatted about the difference between the Windshield and the Bug. About driving defensively and changing lanes. We've discussed car washes and overall cleanliness. We've talked about mentoring. And I hope you've laughed a little, too. At least you came away with the understanding that Dr. Phil is on my speed dial.

In Big "D" with the Kansas Jayhawks

I want to leave you with one more story before we pull into the driveway. It was from the time I was working for KSNW-TV in Wichita. The Kansas basketball team was at the Final Four down in Dallas, Texas. We were going to cover this big story in the Sunflower State, of course, but we didn't have unlimited funds to do so. The station asked Doug, my cameraman, and me to drive to Big "D" instead of taking a jet.

You know me by now; I didn't mind making the eight to nine hour trek south on I-35 from Wichita to Dallas. We left around six in the morning. That meant an even earlier wake-up call. We made good time, pulling into Reunion Arena around 2:30 or so in the afternoon. Just in time to watch the Duke Blue Devils practice. The Jayhawks took the court to work out next.

Afterwards, we did a bunch of interviews. We rushed over to another NBC affiliate to feed what we had for the six o'clock news. Then I went straight to work on a feature story for the ten o'clock show. By the time we finally wrapped up all our work and checked in to the hotel, it was past midnight. We were both exhausted. Spent.

 By the time we finally wrapped up all our work and checked in to the hotel, it was past midnight.

To save the station even more money, Doug and I shared a room. We didn't mind any of these working conditions. We were just thrilled to be there. It was my first Final Four, and Doug was a University of Kansas graduate.

When we got to the hotel, Doug mentioned that he was going to try to grab something to eat. We really hadn't had anything all day. But I was too tired to eat so I went straight to bed.

Now you should know that I generally don't have a problem with sleepwalking. I only remember doing it once before in my life. So it wasn't something that I felt I needed to plan for. I should have.

Doug was off getting a bite to eat, but I crashed immediately. It took me all of five seconds to fall into a deep, satisfying sleep. Sometime in the middle of the night, I found myself standing two inches from a door that read, "Room 1235." Where was I? Was this a dream? What was going on? As I started to shake the cobwebs of my slumber, I began to remember our room number as 1231. Two doors down. I had gotten up to use the facilities. But I was still sleeping. I missed our bathroom by about fifty feet. I had sleep-walked out the door and down the hall. I was standing nose-to-nose with the door to room 1235 when I woke up.

What was I wearing, you ask? Good question. Just my bright red briefs. Not boxers, briefs. No t-shirt, no slippers, no pajamas, and no robe. Just red briefs. Attractive.

I was starting to see things more clearly now. So I kind of chuckled to myself as I ambled down the hall to room 1231. I began to tap lightly on the door. "Hey, Doug, let me in." I whispered so as not to wake the rest of the 12th floor. No answer.

> *To compound things, the original reason for my trip to the hallway was starting to resurface. I really had to go to the bathroom; my bladder was about to burst.*

So I knocked a little more forcefully. "Hey Doug, come on man, let me in!" At this point, I didn't care if I woke up all the adjoining rooms. I just wanted to get back into mine. Still no answer. To compound things, the original reason for my trip to the hallway was starting to resurface. I really had to go to the bathroom; my bladder was about to burst. So now I'm starting to do my little "gotta go" dance up and down the corridor.

I bumped into someone's room service tray out in the hallway and picked up a soup spoon from the remains. Back at Room 1231 I started to bang on the door so hard that the wood was starting to chip away. I got down on my hands and knees and yelled though the slit at the bottom of the door. I felt like Fred Flintstone yelling at Wilma. "DOUG! WAKE UP AND LET ME IN!" I screamed. Still no response from Doug. The only thing I could think was that he was not actually in the room, but still out getting a bite to eat.

I didn't know what time it was. I wasn't wearing a watch. Just the red briefs. I was wishing that I had taped a spare key to my skivvies. I was really at a loss of what to do.

I couldn't exactly go down to the lobby and get another key, not in my condition. I went up and down the entire hallway looking for a house phone so I could call security. I was tempted to knock on anyone's door—I really had to go. And I was running out of effective dances.

Just as I was getting back in front of our room, I heard the distinctive "ding" of the elevator. Someone was coming! For whatever reason, I sort of crouched down covering myself. I didn't know who was going to come around the corner. The best-case scenario of course would be to see my roommate coming around the bend. Then we could both get in the room without too much more embarrassment. No such luck.

It was security. I thought for sure I was going to be hauled off, in cuffs and red briefs, and charged with some crime. "What's going on up here?"

Mister man in the uniform asked. "Half the floor has called and said there's some crazy man in a red bikini in the hallway making all sorts of racket." I had no defense. I was holding the evidence in my hand. A bent, tarnished soup spoon. I quickly tried to explain the situation. He must have read the desperation in my eyes. He had pity on me and let me into Room 1231. First stop, bathroom. After I finished my business, I went back to bed. Passing a sound asleep Doug in the process. Yes, he was there, and he missed the whole show.

One final note. Since that night, I have barricaded every hotel room door from the inside. While sleep-ing fully clothed.

Are you laughing? Good! I was hoping this would be the result as we get home. It's been a terrific ride—

I had a great time. Let's do it again real soon.

Epilogue
Baseball Poetry

As you could tell from this book, I have a deep admiration and respect for the game of baseball. The following really has little to do with the book itself. I just wanted you to have a little added bonus. I'm including a couple of baseball poems I wrote.

The first one, "I Love Baseball," I penned back in 1994. It was the year of the player's strike. Everyone was bashing the game. I agreed that there was plenty wrong, but I still loved baseball. So one night I sat down and wrote some of the reasons I enjoyed the game so much. So when you get frustrated with the overpriced athletes. The drugs. The steroids. The Mitchell Report. Whatever. I invite you to glance at this poem. It may stir something inside to get you back.

The second poem was written during my years with the Rockies. I hope you enjoy them. Again, I sure enjoyed traveling with you.

I Love Baseball

I love baseball!

I love a double in the gap. A relay from the warning track of the outfield. Digging in at the plate. A towering home-run.

I love the outline of the field against the back-drop of the pristine, perfectly mown, green grass.

I love the history of baseball. Each generation compared with the past.

I love the stories from that past. Bobby Thompson's shot heard 'round the world. The story, well come to think of it, any story about the Sultan of Swat Babe Ruth.

The story of a doomed Lou Gehrig playing in more than 2,000 straight games. Then, while knowing his days are numbered, saying, "I consider myself the luckiest man on the face of the earth." I love that.

I love the fact that now, some 60 years later, Cal Ripken of the Baltimore Orioles has played in more consecutive games than the man they called the "Iron Horse."

Oh yes. I love the nicknames in baseball. The Yankee Clipper, Crime Dog, and Mr. October.

I love this game!

I love its smells. The freshly cut grass. A resin bag, a leather glove.

I love the colors of baseball. Purple seats at Coors Field. The Green Monster at Fenway. The Big Red Machine in Cincinnati.

I love the sounds of baseball. The crack of the bat, the pop of the ball in the catcher's mitt. The buzz of the crowd. Organ music. Vendors squawking, "Scorecard, get your scorecard!"

I love baseball, don't you? Don't you just love the strategy, the signs, the diving catches? The bases loaded or a suicide squeeze?

I love the statistics. The records that stand the test of time. Rotisserie Leagues. Little League. Mom's and dad's watching junior try to play like *the* Junior in Cincy. I love Opening Day, the All-Star game and the Fall Classic.

I love baseball's memories. Memories of the pine tar game in New York. Memories of Joe Carter dancing around the bases in Toronto. Memories of the "Called Shot" in Chicago. Memories of Kirk Gibson's fist pump in Los Angeles. I love Sandy Koufax in Dodger blue, the Mick in pinstripes, and the Splendid Splinter in Red Sox.

I love kids playing baseball on the sandlots. Getting caught in a pickle, right field's out. Sa-wing batter! I love baseball! I love sitting in the stands on a warm summer's night keeping score the way my dad taught me.

A man once wrote that baseball is a game for America. He was right then, he's still right.

Baseball, I love this game!

Once Upon a Time

Once upon a time, more that a century ago, more than a Civil War ago, there stood a group of 18 men in a pasture ready to do battle in a very different way.

Once upon a time, those men, farmers and laborers by trade invented what we now call our National Pastime.

Once upon a time, a stick and a crude ball were the only tools used in this new craft. Resin and spikes and even leather gloves were tools for future generations.

Once upon a time, a game so perfect in design, captured a nation. A nation torn apart by the blue and the gray. And now brought together by a ball and a strike.

Once upon a time, there was the Black Sox scandal. And naysayers said the game would never survive, but then...

Once upon a time, there was the Babe. A Sultan of Swat with a swing mightier than any scandal. Babe Ruth changed the game almost single-battingly.

Once upon a time, there was a brave man named Jackie. A man willing to absorb the slings and arrows of a bigoted nation. After Jackie Robinson left his mark, the game could truly be called the National Pastime.

Once upon a time, there was Willie and Hammerin' Hank. The Splendid Splinter and the Mick. Spahn and Sain and pray for rain.

Once upon a time, we suffered through yet another player's strike. Naysayers said the game would never survive, but then...

Once upon a time, there was Big Mac and Sammy Sosa. It was the summer of a home-run derby the likes of which we'd never seen before.

And now? A Mitchell report has thrown baseball from the sports page to the front page. Naysayers will tell you the game can't survive, but then...

Once upon a time, there's always the game. Baseball is more than scandal and strike. Baseball is a man and his son walking hand-in-hand on their way to the park for a little game of catch. With nothing more than a ball and a glove, and a mountain of memories.

About the Author

Dave Armstrong is a Sports Announcer for ESPN and the Big 12 Network. His trademark "Wow!" can be heard on broadcasts throughout the year.

He has announced Big 12 Men's basketball for more than twenty years. He has also been the "voice" of the Kansas Jayhawks on television for more than a decade.

Dave also serves as a Play-by-Play announcer for ESPNU's coverage of College Football.

In addition to all these duties, Dave now encourages and motivates audiences to continue to view a wonderful life through the windshield.

For more information, to book Dave for your event, or to orders books, visit his website at: www.davearmstrongwow.com

Made in the USA